More Walks to Wet your Whistle

A second collection of circular walks, with a pub, in Shropshire and along its Staffordshire Borders

by
Roger Seedhouse

Meridian Books

Published 1999 by Meridian Books

ISBN 1-869922-36-0

A catalogue record for this book is available from the British Library.

Meridian Books
40 Hadzor Road, Oldbury, West Midlands B68 9LA

Printed in Great Britain by MFP Design & Print, Manchester

Contents

Introduction

Perceptions

When it comes to walking, attitudes vary enormously. Some would be filled with dread at the prospect of having to walk half a mile; others would regard a 20 mile trek as little more than a stroll. This publication is aimed at what is probably the vast majority of us who fall somewhere between these two extremes.

Pleasures

You've heard it before but I'll say it again – walking is good for you! It is an inexpensive way to get exercise and allows you to see at close hand the wonderful countryside with which this island is blessed. It is amazing how much hidden beauty there is even on your own doorstep – go out and enjoy it!

Pubs

A pub is not essential for a good walk but the two combine admirably together. Many walkers appreciate a watering hole en route or at the end of a walk – not extremely 'posh' pubs serving expensive meals (walkers don't tend to be popular in such places) but simple country locals where they can take a break and sample the unique character which some of them possess. However, there is no point in having a great pub and an indifferent walk, or vice-versa, and in striking a balance it is inevitable that there will be a mix of pub types, although I have endeavoured to confine the choice to those where the walker will feel at ease.

Points to consider

1. Wear sensible gear. A good pair of boots is essential; so are waterproofs and warm clothing in less clement weather or when undertaking wild hill walks.

2. If you can, take a map of the area. Landranger (1¼ inches to the mile) is the most commonly used but Pathfinder (2½ inches to the mile) is better. I am not suggesting this because you are likely to get lost but merely as a prudent precaution just in case you do stray off the route or if, perhaps because of bad weather, you wish to curtail your walk. A compass is also a useful item for the same reason.

3. Some paths, particularly those less well used, can get overgrown in summer. A walking stick can make life a lot easier in such situations, so can a small first aid kit in the event of a close encounter with a bramble.

4. The countryside is constantly changing. Seasonal changes can make things which appear obvious or easy to recognise in summer less so in winter and vice-versa. Be wary also of physical changes. The position or type of gate/fence/stile may be altered, field boundaries are changed or

even removed altogether, tracks can be diverted (officially or otherwise) etc.

5. Without wishing to state the obvious, give consideration to the choice of time to do a particular walk. Not the time of day necessarily, although you will need to allow adequate time to complete the long walks, but the time of year. You may wish to avoid those walks covering intensively farmed areas during, say, June – August when paths over cropped fields can be a problem. Even though landowners are under a legal obligation to maintain paths after planting, some of them don't. Similarly, I would not advise walking over very hilly country (the Long Mynd, for example) on an iffy winter's day. I have endeavoured to give some guide as to the best times to do the walks in each Factfile.

6. A Right of Way is precisely what it says – you have the right to walk along it at all times unimpeded. Fortunately, most County Councils pursue a continuing programme of clearing and waymarking paths, but this is a huge task and many remain obscure. Likewise, most landowners adopt an enlightened attitude towards walkers but occasionally obstructions will be encountered, paths will have been obliterated or diverted or not reinstated after planting has taken place. Try not to be daunted by such things and remember that you have a legal right to pass. Needless to say, common sense should come to the fore in such situations; for example, it may be more practical to take a path around the edge of a cropped field rather than across it or follow an unofficial diversion rather than stick to the line on the map. Any serious obstructions should, however, be reported to the local council's Rights of Way department – addresses are given on page viii.

7. Some animals can create consternation for the walker. Farm dogs are frequently encountered but mostly make a lot of noise rather than cause any physical injury. Again, a walking stick is useful just to be on the safe side. A field of frisky young bullocks is best avoided. Even though they are merely curious or think you have come to feed them, I prefer to skirt around them where possible. Sheep are no problem!

8. Not many landlords like muddy boots trampling over their floors. Try to be considerate and, if you cannot clean them off, take them off and leave outside or in a lobby.

9. Last, but not least, **REMEMBER THE COUNTRY CODE!**
Enjoy the country and respect its life and work.
Guard against all risk of fire.
Keep dogs under close control.
Keep to public footpaths across farmland.
Use gates and stiles to cross field boundaries.
Leave all livestock, machinery and crops alone.
Take your litter home.
Help to keep all water clean.
Protect wildlife, plants and trees.
Make no unnecessary noise.
Fasten all gates.

The Walks

S HORTER walks are all contained within the route of the main walks and those paths applicable to short routes only are denoted by dots on the sketch maps

Main walks are designed so that the pub break is roughly at the half-way point; shorter routes start and finish at the pub. *Individual circumstances may dictate a change of start point to fit in with public transport or pub opening times.*

Grid references (GR) for the starting points are given in the Factfiles. If you are unfamiliar with the use of these you will find details on Ordnance Survey Landranger maps.

Reference points on the sketch maps are shown in the text thus: **❶**

Public transport services to some areas are very limited or even non-existent – see individual Factfiles for details. In a few cases there is a better service to the start of the shorter walk so, if you are going to do the main walk, you may prefer to start and finish at the shorter starting point. Although public transport details were believed to be correct at the time of going to press you should always check times before setting off. Some appropriate telephone numbers are:

British Rail: 0345-484950
Centro (West Midlands trains and buses): 0121-200 2700
Shropshire Busline: 0345-056785
Staffordshire Busline: 01785-223344
Severn Valley Railway: 0800-600 900 (Talking Pages)

County public transport timetables can be purchased. For details and prices telephone:

Shropshire Public Transport Unit, 01743 253030
Staffordshire Busline, 01785 223344

Details of pub opening times are given in the individual Factfiles. Regrettably, some country pubs now find it necessary to close at certain times, particularly weekday lunch-times, and this might cause some difficulty if you wish to walk at these times. In such cases we suggest that you might like to start at the pub and time your walk to take advantage of evening opening times.

Other than at busy times, most landlords will not object to you leaving a car on their car park if you are going to patronise the pub when you return, but if in any doubt please ask permission.

GOOD WALKING!

About the Author

Roger Seedhouse is a Chartered Surveyor and a partner in a firm of property consultants in the West Midlands. He has lived on the border of Shropshire and Staffordshire all his life and has an extensive knowledge of both counties. When not ministering to the requirements of his two daughters his spare time is divided between Rotary Club activities and walking.

To my wife Lesley and our good friends Mike and Pat Wootton for their tremendous help in the preparation of, and research for, this book.
Thanks also for their assistance to the staff of both Shropshire and Staffordshire Councils' Rights of Way Departments.

If, when using this book, you find any obstructions or problems of access on rights of way it would be very helpful to report these to the appropriate local authority (and to Meridian Books).

The addresses are:

Shropshire:
Rights of Way Section
Leisure Services Department
Column House
7 London Road
SHREWSBURY SY2 6NW

Staffordshire:
Rights of Way Section
Department of Planning and
  Economic Development
County Buildings
Martin Street
STAFFORD ST16 2LE

Publishers' Note

Every care has been taken in the preparation of this book. All the walks have been independently checked and are believed to be correct at the time of publication. However, neither the author nor the publishers can accept responsibility for any errors or omissions or for any loss, damage, injury or inconvenience resulting from the use of the book.

Please remember that the countryside is continually changing: hedges and fences may be removed or re-sited; landmarks may disappear; footpaths may be re-routed or be ploughed over and not reinstated (as the law requires); concessionary paths may be closed. The publishers would be very pleased to have details of any such changes that are observed by readers.

Location Map

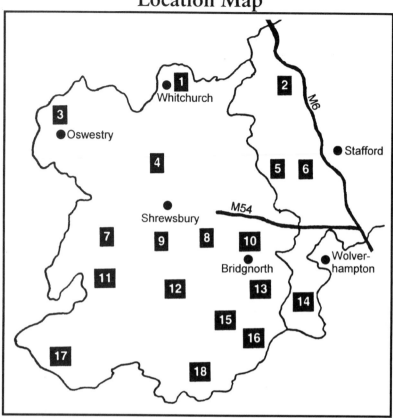

The view from Caynham Camp
(Walk 18)

1
Brown Moss

FACT*file*

MAPS: Landranger 117 & 126; Pathfinder 807 & 828

DISTANCES: 9½ miles; shorter walk 3¾ miles

MAIN START: On lane-side verge to the north of Oss Mere, about 2½ miles to the north-east of Whitchurch, following the minor road towards Marbury from the Town Centre. GR 566443

Public Transport: Nothing convenient.

SHORT START: The White Lion in the village of Ash Magna, about 2½ miles to the south- west of Whitchurch on the road towards Ightfield and Market Drayton. GR 573396.

Public Transport: Limited bus service 218 from Whitchurch stopping at the White Lion.

TERRAIN: Easy walking through open countryside incorporating two Meres, attractive woods and the National Nature Reserve of Brown Moss. Some fields may be planted in the summer months.

THE PUB: The White Lion is a welcoming local with a comfortable atmosphere which will appeal to Real Ale enthusiasts – it was CAMRA recommended in 1995. The bar is festooned with badges, posters and other mementoes of all the guest ales previously served in the pub. Resident beers include Worthington, Bass, Highgate Dark and Checz Lager. There is a good selection of wines by the glass and the bar snacks look quite tempting too, particularly if you like Balti.

Closed at lunchtimes Mon-Thurs (except bank holidays). If you are walking on these days in the summer you may prefer to start from the White Lion to take advantage of early evening opening.

PROCEED eastwards along the lane and 50 yards after passing a new house on your right go over a waymarked stile into a field. Cross directly to negotiate a further stile in the opposite boundary and, in the next field, continue the line forward to another about 150 yards ahead at the eastern edge of Oss Mere. There is a choice of routes here – take the right option along the side of the Mere in rough pasture field. Although much smaller and not so well known as its Ellesmere cousins, Oss Mere is nevertheless a pretty spot – and a lot quieter!

You come to a crossing fence and need to divert slightly left through an opening to continue on course to reach a stile by a gate. Cross into a field and bear right adjacent to a wood which encloses the south end of the Mere. At the end of the field you arrive at a waymarked gate and fence stile BUT DO NOT CROSS. Instead bear left in front of them to follow the long right hedged field boundary for a good quarter of a mile to exit via a stile onto a lane opposite Lodge Farm. ❶

Turn right on the lane and walk along it for about a third of a mile until

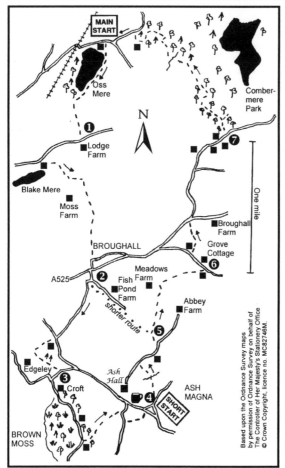

you come to a group of farm buildings on your left, immediately in front of which is a waymarked stile. Cross into a field following the right hawthorn tree boundary with the even smaller Blake Mere over to your right. There is a stile on the right which takes you down to the edge of it if you want to look more closely.

The name Blake is derived from 'black' which is Old English for 'bleached' or 'white' and Mere means 'lake', hence 'white lake', which all goes to prove that black is white! On the south side is the site of the manor house of John le Strange who lived there in the fourteenth century.

Back on course, continue onwards as the boundary loops right to reach a waymarked stile in a crossing hedge.

Once over this proceed forward past a waymark post in the hedge on your right after 80 yards or so, then bear slightly left away from the boundary to a stile in front of an ash tree to the left of a gate. Now cross into a field with a hedge on your left and Moss Farm in view over to the right, and at the top cross another stile and continue ahead on a rough farm track still following the left boundary. As the track swings left into an adjacent field, go straight forward ignoring a stile on your left, to stay with the left boundary which has now changed to hawthorn trees.

At the end of the next field cross a further stile and about 80 yards beyond you will come to a lone oak in the boundary. From here strike half right across the open field to negotiate a stile on the opposite boundary midway between an oak and an ash. In the next field ignore a stile immediately to the right and aim towards the top right corner, thus cutting off the side boundary which weaves in and out with the course of a ditch.

Oss Mere

On gaining the corner you are funnelled through a gateway onto a lane where you bear right between the pretty cottages of Broughall. This in turn exits onto the A525 which is crossed directly into Catteralls Lane. **②**

Keep to the right at a fork after 100 yards and ignore a stile opposite semi-detached houses to continue on the lane for around half a mile before reaching a junction with Ash Road. Turn right then immediately left following a waymark into an agricultural yard by a farmhouse, pass through two gates in quick succession and then walk down a short field passing by what appears to be a helicopter landing pad and hanger. Cross a stile and the next field directly to go through a gate, then bear immediately half left to a small gate in the left side boundary after about 60 yards. Edgeley Hall is now in view over to your right. Once through the gate, head towards a group of fir trees 100 yards ahead and on reaching them follow the field boundary on your left to exit onto a lane. Turn right onto it.

After a short distance keep left at a junction following the sign to Brown Moss and, after passing Croft Cottage, you arrive at an official information board.

BROWN MOSS. *I won't take up space here by repeating what you can easily read – suffice it to say that Brown Moss is one of the most important places for wildlife in the county and is designated a site of special scientific interest. It is home to a number of rare plants and amphibians thrive in the marshes. There is a trail guide showing a route around the other side for those wishing to explore this fascinating area further. If you bear right a little further on, you pass through a car park into the main area of the Moss, a strangely beautiful and tranquil corner.*

Returning to the lane you go by a pair of cottages on your left after which you get a good view of the Moss on the right opposite another car park and after a further 120 yards or so, immediately before reaching some more houses, you come to a waymark where you bear left along a track into a wooded area, ignoring the fork to the right. Continue ahead by a waymark post after 30 yards and a further 120 yards will bring you to another post which directs you around to the left. DO NOT FOLLOW THIS but continue your line more or less directly forward on a narrow path to the edge of the trees where you will find a stile (after only some 20 yards).

Cross and bear right to follow a field boundary and at the end of it cross another stile. In the field now facing you cut half right aiming towards some buildings which you can just see the tops of. This is an upward course which exits onto a lane via a waymarked gate on the far boundary. If the field is planted it may be more practical to follow the boundary around to this point. Turn right and the lane descends through an S-bend, immediately after which look carefully for a waymarked stile on your left. Cross this and another shortly afterwards, then yet another at the end of a short field. Once over this bear half left to cross a double stile which you can see about 150 yards ahead in the opposite boundary. Now follow the left hedged boundary towards the houses of Ash Magna. Cross a stile onto a short track leading to another stile exiting onto a lane. Directly opposite is The White Lion. ❹

ASH MAGNA. *A substantial village on high ground with an unspoilt centre and some attractive old buildings. Ash Hall is a text book eighteenth century Queen Anne style house on the highest point in the village and at the entrance to Ash Grange, a late Victorian mansion now divided into flats, a phantom monk in a flowing hooded habit has been seen. Don't worry that you might encounter the ghost today though – the last sighting was in 1972.*

On overcoming any inclination to take root, leave the pub and turn left up a lane through a residential area keeping left at a junction. After another 150 yards or so take a left turn between bungalows on a tarmac service road leading through a garage compound. Go straight ahead over a stile into a field and veer half right across it aiming just to the right of the corner formed by an adjacent field. You have to cross a little footbridge before getting there and you continue beyond the corner to another footbridge and a stile.

There is a choice of routes here – take the one more or less straight forward on the same line parallel with and about 40 feet away from the left boundary of a field to reach a gate and stile on the opposite boundary. Cross and turn right onto a narrow lane and continue on it as it loops left by a cottage. Shortly after this the lane bears right towards Abbey Farm and, just before it does so, turn left along a waymarked path between rows of trees. Ignore a stile on your right after about 150 yards but a few yards further on you will arrive at a stile in front of you with another choice of routes. ❺

Unless walking the short route take the way to the right through a field to a stile about 150 yards ahead in the opposite boundary. Cross and continue line forward across another, larger, field to a stile on the far side to the left of a short line of trees and hedge and to the right of Meadows Farm. Proceed into the next field following the right boundary as it loops left and then turns sharp right. The route now follows the right boundary for some 120 yards then continues more or less in a straight line cutting off the bottom right corner of the field to a double stile with footbridge on the far boundary. If the field is planted you may have to follow the right boundary around to the same point. Once over, continue with the boundary on your right to cross another stile then carry on the same line to the top right corner of the next field to exit onto Foxes Lane via a stile and small plank bridge, which can be obscured by vegetation in summer.

❻

Turn left, pass Grove Cottage and just before reaching a more modern building there is a waymarked stile on the right. Cross into a field following the left hedged boundary with Broughall Farm in view and, at the end, cross another stile and continue forward following the same boundary hedge. This veers sharp left after about 30 yards but you don't – instead bear just slightly left heading towards a lone oak between the third and fourth house in view ahead (from the left) and on the far boundary you will find a gate to exit onto the A525.

Cross the main road diagonally – and carefully – to enter a lane signed Old Woodhouse. This quiet lane meanders through a sparsely populated agricultural area and you stay on it for a distance of about a mile. Having ignored a turning right after a little under half that distance you pass a house and barns on the left then a detached property immediately afterwards on your right. A short distance on is a waymark on your left but you ignore that too and continue ahead past another house on your right with barns opposite. Another 100 yards or so will bring you to a waymarked path on the left leading into a wood which you take. **❼**

You shortly cross a stile by a lodge and proceed on a grassy path through very attractive mixed woodland. After another 200 yards bear left at waymark (if you reach the end of the wood you've gone too far!) and keep ahead at next the waymark about 100 yards further on. Follow the path for a while as it winds through the wood and at another waymark bear left and then cross a wide fence stile to exit from the wood. Bear left along the top edge of the wood to a waymarked gate. The definitive route suggests passing through the gate and turning right but there is clearly a preferred permissive way as marked which involves turning right in front of the gate to follow an upward course in a field with a timber post boundary on the left.

The panoramic Combermere Park comes into view now through the trees over the Cheshire border to your right. The Mansion is built on the site of a former twelfth century Cistercian Abbey and during the

Napoleonic Wars played host to the Duke of Wellington who was a friend of the then Viscount Combermere.

Bear left through a gate at the top of the field and turn right to continue the line forward but on the left side of the boundary. Where the field ends continue ahead into woodland again to cross a stile and footbridge followed quickly by another stile leading onto a rising path along the left edge of the wood. At a waymarked stile cross and bear right to proceed with the wood on your right until crossing another stile back into the wood again. After a short distance you will exit onto a crossing track and branch left to follow the path as it re-enters the wood yet again but after about 200 yards bear left following a waymark to depart from the main track.

The path now loops right as you approach farm buildings ahead (maybe there should be another waymark here?) and you go with this to keep tight on the fenced boundary along the bottom edge of the wood. Cross a stile and turn right to reach the top of a field where there is another stile exiting onto a lane. Bear left on the lane, which runs along the county border, ignore a turning left after 300 yards to return to the start.

SHORTER WALK

FROM the White Lion, point 4, follow the long route to point 5 and the stile presenting a choice of routes. Take the left option crossing the field diagonally to a waymarked gate in the top corner. Go through into the field opposite following the hedged boundary and brook to exit via a stile onto a tarmac lane. Continue straight ahead on the lane which after a while passes Fish Pond Farm before reaching a junction, with the village of Broughall over to the right. You are now back on the long route at the fork referred to in Catteralls Lane just after point 2. Turn left and follow the long route directions to Brown Moss and back to the pub.

2
Hanchurch Hills

FACT*file*

MAPS: Landranger 118 & 127; Pathfinder 809 & 830

DISTANCES: 9½ miles; shorter walk 3¼ miles

MAIN START: The Hanchurch Hills Car Park which is just off the Drayton Road about one and a half miles south-west of M6 Junction 15. To get there from the Motorway you quickly leave the A500 by turning right at the first island (if approaching from the Stoke-on-Trent or Newcastle directions you will either turn left or continue ahead respectively at the same point) then continue ahead on the A519 at traffic lights after about 300 yards. This road takes you under the motorway but immediately afterwards bear right along Drayton Road and follow it for about a mile before turning left opposite a cottage/shop to the car park.

> **Public Transport:** Nothing to the start point. Limited bus service 350 (Eccleshall/Newcastle) calls at Swynnerton and you could start the walk from there.

SHORT START: As above. This short walk differs from all the others in that it is not centred on the pub. Whilst the countryside around Swynnerton is very nice, I have chosen to route the short walk around the scenic woods of Swynnerton Old Park to the north but have no doubt that you will find a way to visit the Fitzherbert Arms if you wish either before or after the walk.

TERRAIN: A trail through beautiful pine woods and over farmland, visiting two rural villages and return via Hanchurch Hills. Gentle climbs only. Walk at any time.

THE PUB: The Fitzherbert Arms in Swynnerton is a traditional village pub with a bar, lounge and restaurant serving a mouth-watering selection of reasonably priced meals. Bar snacks also available. Ales include Worthington, Boddingtons, Caffreys, Bass, Guinness and Carling. Outside seating.
Normal opening times.

IN the car park is a memorial stone to Lord Stafford in recognition of his dedicating the surrounding area for perpetual enjoyment by the public. From there return to the lane and cross directly following a waymark through a forestry gate onto a broad shale path though pine forest. Ignore all side paths and stay on it for about two thirds of a mile until it narrows and descends to go round a gate. After a further 120 yards or so you emerge at a crossing track in front of a field.

Bear left with the field now on your right and ignore a gate on your left after about 80 yards leading back into the wood and another gate a few yards further on to stay on a path between tree lined banks. This is a frequently used bridleway and can get churned up at times but soon winds

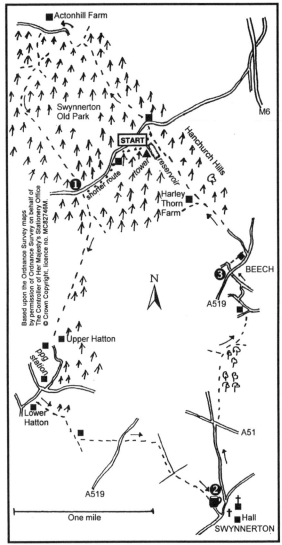

left alongside another field and develops into a tarmac lane. You pass the driveway to Acton Hill Farm on the right and after another 80 yards bear left over a stile to the right of a gate. You quickly cross another stile onto a path leading into Swynnerton Old Park and keep ahead at a fork after 40 yards or so.

The path descends gently and in another 300 yards turn right at a T-junction to arrive at a more complex junction of paths after a further 50 yards. Here bear right along the main gravelly path – not the sharp right downhill – and stay on this now for some time as it takes you through some stunningly beautiful pine forest. The path twists and turns a bit, then straightens into a long avenue to exit via a gate onto a lane. ❶

Cross the lane diagonally following the waymark along a stony track with a field on your left and trees on your right. Ignore a footpath off to the left and continue ahead as the path opens out to pass between fields. This path is known as Common Lane and its pleasant route brings you out at Upper Hatton Farm after a distance of a little over a mile. Go ahead through a gate by the first barn and past the farmhouse on your left to join a tarmac lane.

The lane turns sharp right and passes a magnificent Victorian Pumping Station to meet a junction with the A51. This massive structure is a sister pumping station to the one at Mill Meece, three miles to the south and which is open to the public. Unlike Mill Meece the Upper Hatton station

Upper Hatton Pumping Station

is a shell only, the original steam engines and subsequent diesel generators having been removed some time ago. A modern extension at the rear now pumps water up to Hanchurch Reservoir which you will pass at the end of the walk.

Turn right on the main road along the adjacent side of the pumping station and then bear left down a lane signed Cranberry and Standon. After about 120 yards branch left in front of Lower Hatton Livery Stables along a broad stony track alongside the buildings. Go through a gate at the end of the buildings and stay on the track as it rises, then flattens out to go between some fields. Ignore a waymark to the right and continue past a cottage but, immediately after that, turn left at a waymark post through a gate and along the right edge of a long field.

At the end of the field you emerge onto the A519 and cross it directly onto a public footpath into another field. (*Here note a departure from the route shown on the O.S. map onto a permissive path around the field edge, rather than across it.*). Go through a gap in a crossing boundary and at the end of the next field bear left through another gap to continue on line but now with the field boundary on your right. On meeting a crossing farm track after a further 100 yards turn right onto it and enjoy the expansive views over to your right. You will come to another crossing track and go straight over it following the timber waymark post along a narrow path between hedgerows. A distance of about a third of a mile will bring you out onto a tarmac lane running between houses (Wrekin View) on the outskirts of Swynnerton Village. Continue past the Village Hall, ignoring the waymark opposite, and the lane takes you along the rear of the Fitzherbert Arms. **2**

SWYNNERTON. *The village is dominated by the huge Georgian Hall and its Estate with the Anglican church of St. Mary's and the Gothic style Catholic church opposite each other. The former has a number of interesting features, including a carved oak rood screen, attractive stained glass, a 7ft high statue of Christ and the tomb of John de Swynnerton, a twelfth century crusader. Until the middle 1500s the Swynnerton family were Lords of the Manor but at this time a daughter married a Fitzherbert, the name of the present Lord Stafford. If you recall, at the start of the walk there was a commemorative stone marking the dedication of the surrounding woods to the public by Lord Stafford. The Fitzherberts built the Catholic church. A number of streets and properties are named after various notable villagers over the years, including Bernard Cheadle Close after the blacksmith who warned the Swynnerton family of Cromwell's impending arrival, thus giving them time to escape.*

On leaving the pub turn left and after 100 yards left again along a lane signed Beech, Stableford and Newcastle. There are spectacular views on each side over open countryside and over Stoke-on-Trent to the right. After half a mile you reach a junction with the A51.

Turn right and cross carefully to go almost immediately left along a waymarked bridleway through a gate onto a broad stony track. This shortly becomes more grassy and you pass to the left of a deciduous wood with good views to the left and again towards Stoke on the right over the trees. You arrive at a timber waymark and ignore a turning left to continue on a descending course between trees. After 120 yards or so fork left following a waymark along a narrow path between rows of mixed trees. Unfortunately, you may be able to hear the M6 at this point.

Eventually, after a gentle rise, you reach a junction with a wider track and turn right onto it alongside a cottage. After a short distance bear left at another junction on a lane between attractive properties in the village of Beech. Another 120 yards will bring you to a fork and here branch right on a pretty downhill section of lane to reach another lane where you turn left uphill to pass under the A519. ❸

The lane continues to rise and reaches a point where it sweeps left and here you leave it by turning 90 degrees right following a waymark down a stony track. This takes you to the left of a large white painted residence to exit onto another lane where you turn left. You immediately pass a mobile phone station and get another view of Stoke on the right. A distance of a third of a mile or so will bring you to a pair of cottages, one of which is called Harley Thorne Cottage, where there is a junction. Keep straight ahead, effectively taking the right option, and depart from the Hanchurch Walk waymarks to go round a metal gate onto a broad stony track with Harley Thorne Farm over to your left.

This is a pleasant path running along fringe woodland to the Hanchurch Hills. You pass to the right of Hanchurch Reservoir with its Victorian Water Tower and go round a gate to continue ahead to return to the start.

SHORTER WALK

FROM the start point of the main walk follow it through to point 1, the exit from Swynnerton Old Park. Turn left along the lane and after about a third of a mile look for a kissing gate on your right just after a cottage. Go through and immediately fork left onto a rising stony path. This is fairly steep and at the top you cross a picnic area and the car park beyond to meet the corner fence of a Victorian Water Tower by Hanchurch Reservoir. Now keep on the main track back to the car park.

The lane to Beech

3
Selattyn

FACT*file*

MAPS: Landranger 126; Pathfinder 827

DISTANCES: 8 miles; Shorter walk 4½ miles

MAIN START: Small public car park with picnic tables on the left side of the approach to Graignant village on the B4579, 1½ miles NW of Selattyn which itself is about 3½ miles NW of Oswestry. GR 254350

> **Public Transport:** Frequent servicies into Oswestry but there is not a practical service out to Graignant.

SHORT START: The Cross Keys in Selattyn. GR 267340.

> **Public Transport:** As above, nothing convenient. The regular 2/2A Wrexham-Oswestry service stops at Hengoed (Mon-Sat), about 1½ miles east of Selattyn.

TERRAIN: Undulating and scenic Welsh border country with sections along the historic Offa's Dyke path. A few climbs but nothing too arduous. Walk at any time.

THE PUB: What a super little walker friendly pub the Cross Keys is. Oozing quaintness, it has two small bars with beamed ceilings and almost feels as though it is part of someone's house. In reality it is and might at first appear to be closed until you discover the back entrance. Ales include Banks's, Guinness and Wrexham Lager. Pleasant beer garden.

The pub is closed at lunchtimes Monday-Friday but the landlord will open up on these days if required and he is there. A telephone call beforehand would be advisable – 01691 650247.

ROM the car park turn right towards Selattyn and after 150 yards almost double back sharp right up a broad surfaced track waymarked Offa's Dyke Path. The way climbs quite steadily and you continue ahead at a stile and again at a waymark along a grassy section. After a while the path opens out into a field and you cross another stile before bearing half left at a waymark 50 yards further on. Here follow a narrow track across an open field roughly parallel with a hedge line and then a belt of fir trees on your left.

As you reach the top of a crest wonderful views open up over the Welsh Border Hills towards Llansilin. You will cross a stile after another 300 yards or so following the acorn symbol for Offa's Dyke Path keeping to the right hand boundary down a narrow path between bracken. Cross a further stile after 200 yards then another after a similar distance and bear right along the waymarked driveway towards Orseddwen Farm. You leave it after a few yards at the next waymarked stile following the acorn across a short section of field to go over yet another stile after 30 yards.

Continue in the next field with a dry stone wall on your right, down a

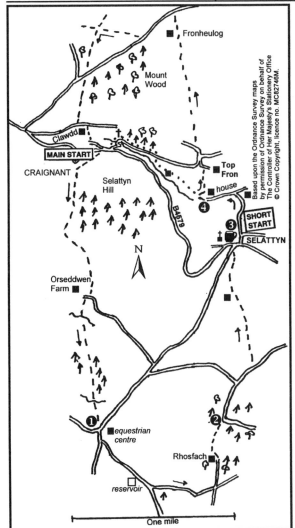

dip and over a foot-bridge – well it makes a change from a stile! The embankment on the far side leads you over a ladder stile and into a field where you continue the line forward along the right boundary heading for a small conifer wood. Cross a further stile and another before entering a narrow path running alongside the right edge of the wood between trees and a fence. You will pass by an attractive row of Scots Pine standing like sentinels overlooking the countryside to the right before exiting the wood via a stile. Are all these stiles making you notice your leg muscles yet?

Continue ahead along the right boundary of a rough field and after about 100 yards the ground dips to a footbridge. Cross this and proceed with the bank of Offa's Dyke on your right. In 200 yards cross a stile into the next field and keep to the right boundary heading towards farm buildings. Another stile will bring you onto a lane. Carved on this stile is some encouraging news for walkers – there are only 127 miles to go to Chepstow! **❶**

Turn right on the lane and follow it as it curves left around Oswestry Equestrian Centre (signed Old Racecourse and Llawnt). In 150 yards bear left along the Oswestry road and stay on this as it rises, then flattens out to pass a covered reservoir on your right. Shortly after that, as the road descends, take the left turn along an unsigned minor lane. When you come to a crossing track after about a third of a mile branch left towards Rhosfach and, on reaching the farm buildings, continue almost directly ahead on a grassy track between a wooden barn and a stone wall.

At the end of this track you arrive at two metal gates with a stile between them – cross into the right hand field turning immediately left to reach another metal gate. Go through, bearing right along the field edge passing a small corrugated barn and descend following a line of trees on your right (not the fence line) to cross a fence stile into a cleared area of woodland sloping down into a valley. You can see a road below – this is your destination. The way is directly ahead on the same line down to meet the road but, at the time of research, there was a winding path cut through the remains of the felled trees taking you down to the same point and it would seem to be sensible to follow this route. On reaching the road turn left onto it. ❷

After perhaps a little less than a quarter of a mile bear right at a junction towards Weston Rhyn and Oswestry. Superb views now open up ahead and to the right and after another quarter of a mile, just before the lane starts to descend more sharply, look for two gateways on your left. Take the first of these onto a stony track along the right boundary of a field and follow it as it rises gradually and becomes more grassy.

At the top pass through a gate into another field and continue your line forward alongside the right boundary to pass through two further gates before approaching a house ahead. Press forward towards the house which, at the time of research, was undergoing extensive refurbishment and you will find a waymarked metal gate to the left of it. DO NOT GO THROUGH but turn right through a gateway in the field corner and down a path alongside the right of the house. This path can get overgrown in summer but descends and broadens out to meet a junction with a lane. Turn right then left at a road junction into Selattyn and the Cross Keys. ❸

SELATTYN. *Visitors to Selattyn will appreciate its charming character and peaceful setting. It wasn't always so of course – this is border country and the scene of constant warfare through the ages. Stones at the side of the Dyke mark the sites of soldiers' graves. The legendary Owain Glendwr, and the scourge of Henry IV and Henry V, was said to have sheltered on Selattyn Hill which overlooks the village. If you have the time visit the Church of St. Mary the Virgin, an immaculately restored and maintained building with a fifteenth century barrel roof and lovely stained glass as well as many other interesting artefacts.*

Reluctance to leave might prove quite strong but when persuaded to do so turn left, then left again along a lane signed Weston Rhyn. After about 100 yards, where the lane bears right, continue ahead along a narrow lane to the left of a cottage. Ignore a public footpath sign on your left after 150 yards and descend to cross two stone bridges in quick succession, after which there is a short climb to a junction by a white cottage. Turn left here and where the tarmac ends by a house continue ahead on a stone track for

40 yards before cutting right up a narrow path leading around the rear of the house. ④

On reaching a junction at the top, turn left to continue the ascent on a path which can at times be overgrown, passing the attractive Top Fron farmhouse on the right to exit onto a lane. Bear left to meet a crossroads after 50 yards and continue directly across, hopefully not failing to notice the magnificent views to your right. After a further 120 yards the lane swings left and here you go forward through a gate onto a broad track.

After a few yards stop at a gateway on the right – there is an expansive view over a huge swathe of countryside to the north. Weston Rhyn is off to the right and further to the north is Chirk, which from this angle appears dominated by its massive chipboard factory. Back on track, continue along the field edge following the right boundary. There is a track between hedgerows which is the official right of way but if this is too overgrown you will probably have to go through a gap in a crossing boundary and continue along the field edge.

You will go through a gate and at the next field boundary cross a stile by a timber gate to carry on forward across another field to a further stile. Here we are directed onto the enclosed track whether we like it or not and you pass along an avenue of ash trees, although other species have grown up between them. Admire the super views before eventually arriving at Fronheulog Farm and cross a fence stile to the right of it to pass over a small field to a gate on the opposite boundary (permissive path). Go though this and turn right onto a stone driveway leading away from the farm to exit at a lane, then turn left onto it. As you are walking along views open up on the right of Chirk Castle and again in several places further on.

Owned by the National Trust, Chirk Castle is a splendid Marcher

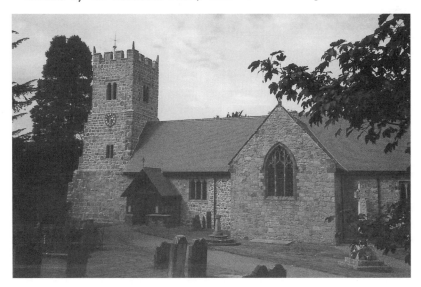

Church of St Mary the Virgin, Selattyn

fortress strategically located to command extensive views over the surrounding countryside. It was completed in 1310 and contains numerous features of interest including some elaborate plasterwork. It is open to the public but check times before planning a visit.

After about a quarter of a mile you come to the corner of Mount Wood on your left and directly opposite is a broad track. Bear right onto this track which narrows to pass between an area of small trees to reach a junction with Offa's Dyke Path with stiles to right and left. Take the left alternative into a field and follow the right boundary to exit via a stile onto a lane. Cross the lane directly to continue on Offa's Dyke Path, this section of which forms the boundary between Shropshire and Clwyd and actually involves walking on top of the ridged earthworks.

OFFA'S DYKE. *A coast to coast long distance path, running the length of the England-Wales border. The Dyke was built in the late eighth century by the King of Mercia to define a frontier between his kingdom and the various Welsh kingdoms to the west, and to control trade. The earth bank was generally about 6ft high and 60ft wide and ditched, usually on the west side, although there are variations in construction probably as a result of each landowner along the route having responsibility for work on his own section. Of the 81 miles of earthworks that can be traced today, 60 are contained within one unbroken stretch between Knighton and Chirk and you are on part of that now.*

Go over a stile in a crossing fence and then another to exit onto a lane. Bear left and after about 200 yards, just past the entrance drive to 'Clawdd', cut right to continue on a narrow path descending into a valley. You pass the stone built Yew Tree Farmhouse after which the path becomes metalled. At a T-junction turn left, and at the junction with a wider lane bear right back to the starting point.

SHORTER WALK

STARTING from the Cross Keys, point 3, follow the long route *almost* to the end of the walk where you meet a 'junction with a wider lane'. Instead of turning right here bear sharp left down another lane as if you were walking along the second arm of a V which comes to a point at the wider lane referred to. You will descend through an S-bend between a cottage and a tiny stone built chapel and then continue along this pretty lane through fringe woodland with a brook below for some of the way. The route departs from the lane after about half a mile in total and you will need to look carefully for the right path. There is a track off to the left going into the wood (this is just a marker so don't actually go onto it) and about 80 yards after that look for a stile on your right, just after the lane starts a gradual rise.

Cross the stile into a steep field with a dry stone wall on the right and after 30 yards you meet a track and turn left onto it. After another 150 yards or so cross a further stile in a crossing fence above a farmhouse and continue the line forward for 60 yards to join and continue ahead on the driveway going away from the farm. This continues through two gates on either side of some cottages, then passes through two more gates to emerge at a junction with a tarmac lane. You are now back at point (4) and, hopefully, will be able to navigate your return to the Cross Keys. However, in case of memory lapse bear right onto the lane (effectively continue ahead) and after about 300 yards take the first lane off it to the right. Descend and cross the two bridges, then stay on the lane as it climbs to meet a junction. Continue forward on the wider lane for the short distance back to Selattyn.

The Cross Keys, Selattyn

4

Myddle

FACT*file*

MAPS: Landranger 126; Pathfinder 848

DISTANCES: 6½ miles; shorter walk 3½ miles

MAIN START: In lay-by for about three cars by a pool just to the west of Alderton on the road to Myddle. Approach from Shrewsbury is via the A528 to Harmer Hill where you fork right along the B5476 towards Wem. After about 1½ miles take a left turn at crossroads towards Myddle and the lay-by is on your right after a further third of a mile. GR 493238

   Public Transport: Nothing to Alderton. Limited bus service 511 (Shrewsbury/Wem) stops at Yorton half a mile to the east.

SHORT START: The Red Lion in Myddle off the A528, 2½ miles north-west of Harmer Hill. GR 469239.

   Public Transport: Limited bus service 501 from Shrewsbury stops at Myddle.

TERRAIN: Generally easy going over open countryside with no climbs of any significance. Some fields may be planted in the summer months.

THE PUB: The Red Lion is an attractive period building with a comfortable interior to match, with beamed ceilings and fireplace. There is a lounge and bar where both snacks and meals are available and a plaque on the bar proudly boasts an award for its steak and kidney pies. Ales on offer include Banks's, Marstons and Guinness. Various ciders are available on draught such as Woodpecker and Strongbow.

Normal opening times

FROM the lay-by, turn right towards Myddle and after 100 yards there is a waymark directing you left across the bottom corner of a field to a stile 150 yards ahead in a crossing boundary. Go over this and follow a waymark half left across the top corner of the next field aiming for a point about two thirds of the way along a line of trees in view. (If this field is planted you may wish to consider walking around the edge of it) You will see a section of fencing in front of the trees and in it there is a stile to the left of an oak and with a pool off to your left. Cross the stile and bear right for 15 yards before crossing another stile into a field to follow its right boundary of mixed trees.

There is a farm in view off to the left and you will come to another pool on your right. Continue to follow the field edge to the far side of it, then strike out straight across the field to a stile alongside a gate in the crossing boundary 50 yards ahead, with farm buildings in the background. Once over this continue the line forward to the left of a post and wire fence before joining a farm track to exit via a gate onto a lane. Turn left to walk along the lane for about a quarter of a mile through the rural hamlet of Newton on the Hill. Immediately after the last house on the right go through a waymarked gate. ❶

You will cross a stile after 100 yards into a large field, initially passing to the left of a group of fir trees, then following a hedged boundary to exit via a stile onto the A528. Turn left along the grass verge for 25 yards only before crossing the road carefully in front of a sandstone cottage. Take the waymarked path to the left of the cottage and shortly cross a dilapidated stile into a field where you turn right to follow the boundary of it. After 100 yards or so the boundary swings right and here you continue the line more or less straight ahead across the field to meet a belt of trees and a stone wall boundary.

Bear right now on a path along the field edge, cross a stile after about 150 yards and proceed ahead, cutting off the left corner of a field towards a mounded reservoir in view. There are expansive views to the left here over the border hills around Welshpool – on a clear day that is – and to the right over the North Shropshire countryside. Cross another stile to the left of the reservoir onto a narrow path leading to yet another on the far side and continue in the next field to reach a fence stile in front of some more trees 100 yards ahead.

Please pay careful attention to directions on this next section – enter the wood alongside a former sandstone quarry, cross a stile and gently descend on a path with the quarry on your left. At the end of the quarry don't take the steeply descending path to the left but gently climb directly ahead for a short way. As the path levels out you come to a fork where you keep left for about 30 yards before keeping left again at another fork. This route

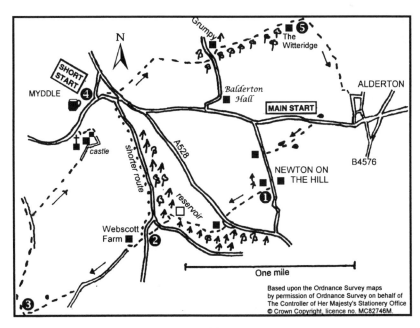

One mile

Based upon the Ordnance Survey maps by permission of Ordnance Survey on behalf of The Controller of Her Majesty's Stationery Office © Crown Copyright, licence no. MC82746M.

then curves right and drops rapidly down a slippery gully (*please take care*) to emerge via a stile onto a lane.

To the left of the stile you may be able to see the remnants of a rock dwelling in the sandstone cliff. Cross the lane directly, negotiating a stile on the opposite side, and go ahead over a field to a further stile in the far boundary after 50 yards. In the next field follow the hedged boundary on your right and go through a gateway onto a lane in front of Webscott Farm.

2

Enter the concrete driveway to the left of the farm buildings. At the rear of the barns but before reaching the farmhouse there are two gates on the left. Take the right hand gate onto a tarmac lane which you will stay with for some time. To begin with the lane is straight but eventually it wiggles right then left. About 100 yards after the left wiggle there is a gate on your right at the end of a short section of hedgerow. The way is now through the gate and across the bottom section of a field, gradually moving away from the left boundary to cross into the next field where you continue the same line alongside the boundary passing a pool on your right. Continue with it as it loops right and winds around the top boundary to a gate between trees to exit onto a farm track. *The right of way here cuts across the top corner, from where the boundary wiggles right, to reach the said gate, but it does seem eminently more sensible to follow the field edge.* **3**

Turn right on the track which twists and turns for a little over half a mile and can get muddy at times. Look for a footpath sign and footbridge on your right and cross into a large field turning half left towards a gate on the far boundary leading onto a track to the right of a hedgerow. You can now just see the top of Myddle Church off to the left. Follow the track until you go through another gate onto a concrete driveway and stay on this as it curves right to go through a waymarked gate, then sweeps left into a farmyard. (On your left here you can see the remains of Myddle Castle – see below.) Don't follow the drive between buildings but look for a waymarked double gate in front of a large barn. Go through this, turn right then immediately left around the rear of the barn before going through another gate on the left at the end of the barn onto a short concrete driveway along the back end of the barn and to the right of sandstone farm buildings… Phew, explaining the way around this barn takes some doing!

After about 50 yards go through yet another gate and continue forward still with sandstone buildings on the left onto a grassy track for another 80 yards or so to exit via a further gate onto the farm driveway facing the church. Turn right up to the road and turn right again into the village to find the Red Lion. **4**

MYDDLE *is a real mixture of ancient and modern with attractive period buildings sitting not altogether comfortably alongside much newer properties. The village has Saxon origins and was known as 'Muelleht' which meant wood by the junction of a stream. The castle was built by Lord Lestrange of Knockin but fell into ruin in the early sixteenth century whilst in the stewardship of an outlaw known as*

Wild Humphrey Kynaston and there is not a lot of it left. At the time of research the church was closed for major restoration work and installation of central heating but it has a long history going back to 1086 and the Domesday Book. The present structure was built in 1744 as a plaque close to the entrance tells us.

Myddle Church

Having accomplished the difficult task of parting company with the pub, turn left and where the road bears right after 125 yards cut left up a surfaced and partly stepped pathway between houses to reach the A528 again at the top. You have now conquered Myddle Hill without oxygen! Cross the road and a waymarked stile opposite to enter a very large field which may be cropped at times. Your route is almost straight across but to help you navigate the uncharted expanse, bear just right of a small wooded hollow and pass to the right of the middle of three lone trees in the field. A stile in the far boundary hedge can be seen immediately to the right of a hawthorn bush.

Cross the stile to turn 90 degrees right and follow the right field boundary of the adjacent field towards a small wood in view. Balderton Hall is off to the right and looks to be an establishment of some status. When level with it you cross a stile into the small wood on a narrow path which exits onto a lane after only 50 yards or so in front of a house with the intriguing if somewhat off-putting name of 'Grumpy'. I imagine that there must be a very good reason or origin for such a name.

Turn right here then left after 20 yards down a broad stone bridleway alongside Grumpy. Just beyond the house the track bears right and you stick with it along the left edge of a narrow coppice. Ignore a bridleway sign on the right to arrive at a cottage called The Witteridge just as the trees end. Continue forward along a grass track and after about 250 yards, just beyond a redundant brick structure now used as a sheep shelter, the path narrows between hedgerows to reach a bridleway sign and gate. **5**

On the gate is a descriptive notice about access and permissive footpaths in the area, courtesy of the Countryside Commission. You do not want to follow the permissive path to Bilmarsh so go through the gate and after 25 yards turn right through another gate into a field; cut off the left side of it by aiming for a gap in the tall hedge on the opposite boundary and go through into the next field. Follow the post and wire boundary on your left, climbing gently until you go through a gate at the top to walk along another field edge as it kinks left then right. After a further 200 yards the boundary kinks again, this time right then left before reaching a gateway in the corner. Here turn left onto a wide farm track and stay with it into the settlement of Alderton. Bear right at the junction with a metalled lane by a farm through this tucked away little community and on reaching the 'main' road, turn right for 300 yards back to the starting point, taking particular care at the blind right hand bend!

SHORTER WALK

FROM the Red Lion, point 4, turn left as if on long route but do not cut left up the path between houses. Instead, continue on the road to the top of Myddle Hill and just before reaching a junction with the A528 turn right down a lane through a pleasant residential area. Ignore a footpath sign on the left leading into a wood and stay on the lane until it passes Myddle sandstone quarry and then a little sandstone cottage just beyond. A few yards further on bear right at a fork along a lane signed Bowmere Heath and in another 200 yards branch right at Webscott Farm along a concrete driveway to pick up the long route at point 2. Now follow the text through point 3 and back to the pub.

5
Norbury Junction

This walk links at Norbury Junction with walk No. 6 Ranton Priory, so you could plan a twenty mile endurance tester if you wish!

FACT*file*

MAPS: Landranger 127; Pathfinder 849

DISTANCES: 10 miles or 7¾ miles; shorter walk 3¾ miles

MAIN START: Any convenient place in Forton Village which is situated about 1½ miles north-east of Newport on the A519 Eccleshall Road. By the church would be suitable if a service is not in progress or likely to be. If so, there is a small lay-by further down the lane on the left. GR 755213

> **Public Transport:** There are good bus services to Newport but there is, at present, nothing really practical to Forton.

SHORT START: The Junction Inn at Norbury Junction. From the Newport direction continue on the A519 through Forton and Sutton then, after another mile turn right to go through Norbury village and on to Norbury Junction after a further three quarters of a mile. From the Eccleshall direction the turning is left some 1½ miles after Woodseaves. GR 793228

> **Public Transport:** Limited services from Stafford or Newport, some of which call at Norbury Junction; others only go as far as Norbury. Advisable to check routes/times.

TERRAIN: Mainly well used paths through pleasant countryside, taking in the largest natural mere in the region, parts of the Shropshire Union Canal and country villages. Walk at any time. Some fields may be planted in summer, and parts can get muddy.

THE PUB: The Junction is located in a picturesque setting on a canal marina, a popular stopping place for boat people. You will normally be greeted by a reception committee of various ducks (outside I hasten to add) and there is a quaint craft shop which is well worth a visit. Inside the pub are two bars and a restaurant where you can get good value snacks or meals. Ales on offer include Marstons, Banks's, Guinness, Murphy's, Carlsberg and Stella Artois. There is also usually a guest beer. If you don't mind the ducks there is outside seating where you can watch the almost constant activity in the marina.
Normal opening times

FORTON. *A pretty little village with a great pub, The Swan, which although not featured on the walk is highly recommended for a visit. It is a pity about the main road which tends to spoil the rural tranquillity somewhat. Forton Hall, next to the church, is a stone gable house of Jacobean appearance but is dated 1665. The church itself is an interesting contrast between the medieval square tower and north aisle and the Georgian nave.*

W ITH your back to the church turn left and, at the end of the churchyard wall, follow the waymark across a stile then through a gate, where there is a choice of routes. Take the option branching half right alongside a line of oak trees. A few yards after the last tree there is an electricity pole with a waymark on it and here bear right along a ridged track and through a gate to cross the disused line of the Newport arm of the Shropshire Union Canal.

Keep following the waymarks until you reach two small metal gates, after which turn left to walk along the hedged edge of a field. After about 50 yards there is another waymark on a post directing you right across the open field to a gateway on the opposite boundary. Go through and continue ahead across the centre of a large, open and sometimes rather squidgy field heading towards Thistleyfield Covert but aiming for a small metal gate about 50 yards to the right of it.

There is a plaque here telling you about Aqualate Mere although you cannot see the Mere at this point. Unfortunately, due to restricted public access, it is difficult to see a lot of it from any point but there is an opportunity a little later on. Once through the gate bear left towards the

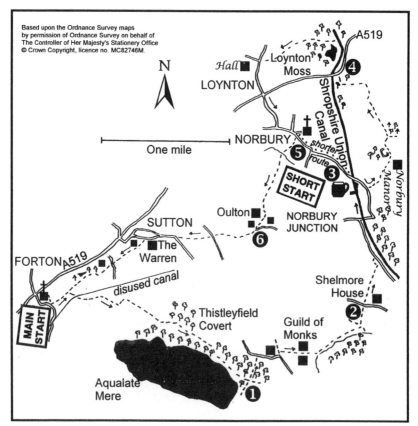

side of the wood and then continue with it on your left to go through another gate at the end. Now proceed directly forward gradually closing with the wooded area around the Mere on your right. You are accompanied by a post and wire fence and where this swings left stay on your line to a dilapidated gate in front of the wood about 100 yards ahead. DO NOT GO THROUGH THE GATE but bear left in front of it and around a wooded mound on your right.

The way shortly brings you to a gateway which now takes you into the wood. Follow the narrow path going off to the right through attractive mixed woodland and after a while the path wiggles around the right hand side of a small hill. You can just catch a glimpse of the Mere from this point through the trees, although in summer even this may be obscured. Exit the wood via a gate and continue forward with the trees on your left and after about 200 yards go through another gate onto a broad crossing track. **❶**

The way is left here through another gate and back into the wood but, if you would like to get a better view of the Mere and possibly sight of some water birds if you have binoculars, turn right for about 200 yards. Aqualate is the largest of the natural meres in the West Midlands region and has long been a secluded haven for wildlife and important for its many species of birds, plants and insects. There is no access other than by public rights of way and this is as close as you are able to get.

Back on the route with the track which rises through the wood and exits onto a broad path between hedgerows to meet a gated junction with a lane, where you turn right. A distance of some 250 yards will bring you to a pair of semi-detached cottages and you bear left immediately after them along a broad stony track but only for 20 yards before branching right along another track opposite the rear gardens of the cottages.

You will shortly arrive at a farm with the fascinating name of 'Guild of Monks'. I have tried to find out the origin of this name but so far without success – if any local historians have the answer please do let Meridian Books know. Pass between the farm buildings and skirt to the right of a large barn to follow a course in a field parallel with and about 25 yards away from the left hedged boundary. On one of my research visits here this area was very muddy indeed. You will see a footbridge about 200 yards ahead on your right – aim for that but do not cross it. Instead, bear left to the corner of the field and cross a waymarked stile to continue in the adjoining field to the left of a hedge.

Next go through a gap in a crossing boundary and press on in another (large) field to a point where the hedge does a little kink. There is a waymarked stile here to cross before continuing on the same line but with the boundary hedge now on your left. As you come to a hedge in front of you, curve right with it and find a waymarked stile in it just to the right of a large ash tree. There are two waymarks here – follow the lower one directing you half left across and up an undulating field. At the top of the rise you can see two farmhouses – aim for the one on your left to reach a gateway in the top left corner to exit onto a lane. **❷**

Cross the lane directly down a broad and sometimes muddy track to the left of Shelmore House. You will pass through a gate and after another 200 yards take the right of two facing gates onto a grassy path between hedgerows. Go through a further gate and continue the line forward in a field to reach a renovated farmhouse. You pass just to the left of it and bear left to follow a brick wall on a course which loops right along a grassy track and up an embankment to exit via a gate onto a lane. Turn left here and after about 300 yards look carefully for a stile on the right leading you into a wood and up an embankment to the Shropshire Union Canal. Bear left onto the towpath and follow it for around half a mile through to Norbury Junction Marina, so named because it was located at the junction of the Shrewsbury and Liverpool and Birmingham sections of the Shropshire Union Canal. Cross over the bridge to reach 'The Junction Inn' ❸

THE SHROPSHIRE UNION CANAL. *Engineered by Thomas Telford (who sadly died during its construction in 1834) the 'Shroppie' was the last of the great narrow boat canals to be built in England. Typified by deep cuttings and high embankments it took ten years to complete but never made a profit due to increasing competition from the railways. It was eventually taken over by London North Western Railway and fell into commercial disuse before the end of the last war.*

When you are able to conquer any overwhelming desire to remain in the bar, leave the pub to join the lane alongside. You can if you wish cut short the main walk at this point by turning left along the lane for about half a mile before turning right at a junction and around towards the village of Norbury. As you enter the residential area, and before reaching the driveway up to the church on your right, look for a timber waymark post in the hedge on the right directing you left on a path between modern houses. This is point (5) and you can follow the remainder of the main walk from there back to the start.

Those intending to go all the way should turn right on the lane over the canal bridge and past the British Waterways maintenance depot. After about 200 yards bear left along the concrete driveway to Norbury Manor. You pass in front of the sandstone house and, shortly after that, the remains of a moat on the left. There is a waymarked opening here and, although the right of way is now across the facing field, it is probably more sensible to keep to the track and it does seem to be the intention that you should.

Continue then on the concrete driveway around the field to arrive at a fork at the corner of a wood. Bear left here on a broad stony track which winds through attractive countryside and eventually passes a wooded area 100 yards to the left before swinging right to meet a waymark and notice on a tree advising you that this is a permissive path. Again it is a more sensible alternative to crossing open fields. Shortly afterwards you exit onto the A519 via a gateway. ❹

Turn left over the canal bridge, then immediately right down an embankment onto the towpath. If you look back along the towpath you will see the curious sight of a telegraph pole at high level on a platform under the bridge. This is called ' High Bridge' or 'Bridge No. 39' and the pole is a survivor of the many lines which once existed on the canal banks. Proceed along the towpath for a quarter of a mile to the next bridge, on both sides of which are metal rope posts with deep grooves worn into them from ages of use. Go under the bridge and bear left up an embankment after 20 yards. At the top turn right in front of Loynton Moss. There is a stile opposite leading you into the reserve should you wish to explore it and a plaque provides details of the flora and fauna to be found there. A marked route enables visitors to see the reserve whilst minimising disturbance to the wildlife so please keep to the paths.

Otherwise or afterwards, continue on the main track which shortly opens out into a field wedged between woods. Keep close to the left edge and on reaching the end of the wood, join a broad track and proceed along it in the direction more or less straight ahead to the right of a line of trees with a ditched brook below. Do not be tempted to turn left along the track leading down the adjacent side of the wood. After about a third of a mile you exit onto a tarmac lane and turn left onto it.

Along this lane you get panoramic views over surrounding countryside and can see the Georgian Loynton Hall if you look back over to your right. On coming to the A519 after some quarter of a mile, cross it directly and carefully towards the village of Norbury. When you reach a junction bear left by some picturesque cottages, pass Norbury House Farm on the right and ignore a turning to the left. After passing a phone box at the entrance to the lane leading to the church, continue for about 50 yards and look for a timber waymark post in the left side hedge directing you right on a path between modern houses. ❺

Cross a stile into a field continuing forward but slightly to the left round an oak tree to another oak on the opposite boundary. Here there is an awkward little double fence stile to cross before bearing half right across a larger field to reach a waymarked gate on the far side which leads you over a footbridge into another field. Now bear half left cutting off the left corner of the field to another waymarked gate after 50 yards or so. Once through, keep parallel with the right boundary, although the exact line moves very gradually away from it and on the far boundary you should arrive at a waymarked fence stile at a point some 20 yards in from the top right corner.

Cross the stile into another large field, bearing half left across it aiming to the left of some farm buildings which come into view. If the field is planted you may be forced to walk around the edge. Do not go to the top left corner but look for and cross a fence stile in the crossing boundary on your left. Now cross the adjacent field and negotiate another fence stile before continuing more or less straight forward, cutting off the top right corner of the next field towards brick farm buildings. Exit via a waymarked gate to immediately cross a broad farm track and a stile into an undulating field with Oulton Farm on your right.

Cross another fence stile on the far side into the next field keeping to the left of the buildings along the top edge. You pass an attractive Victorian farmhouse to reach a small waymarked metal gate leading down an embankment towards two cottages at the base, called Oulton Firs and Rock Cottage. On arrival at a waymarked crossing track turn right onto a gravelled path. **❻**

The path turns to grass almost straight away and you go through a gate into a field following the left boundary. Go through another gate and continue forward through an opening into the next field still following the left boundary. Where the boundary kinks left stay straight ahead to a gate on the opposite side of the field to exit onto a lane. Cross the lane diagonally, then a stile to bear half right, cutting off the bottom right corner of a field to pass through a gap between the first and second trees in a line (reading from the right). Then continue the line forward across the next field to the opposite boundary where there is a stile. Continue the line again across the next field to exit onto a lane via a gate.

Turn right on the lane towards the village of Sutton. It loops left when it reaches the outskirts of the village, then bears right by a house called The Warren. Immediately after that there is a timber waymark post in the right verge directing you left into a concreted yard area adjacent to some recent barn conversions, part of which bears the date 1860. Go through into a pasture field keeping to the right boundary. Cross a fence stile into the next field and, after a further 50 yards, go over a stile into another field where you proceed with the boundary on your left.

A renovated house comes into view ahead and you gradually move away from the left boundary in its general direction to cross a wide track to the left of it (which leads up to the house). Continue ahead, following the waymark on a post taking you to the right of a hedged boundary with the adjacent field. Go through a gate in a crossing boundary and descend to meet the corner of a small wood where there is a stile. Cross and follow a path around to the left of the trees, cross a waymarked stile and continue until reaching a pool on the right. At this point start to move away from the wooded area across the bottom corner of a pasture field to a waymarked gap in a crossing boundary. Now proceed forward to join the line of trees encountered at the beginning of the walk and retrace your steps the short distance back to the starting point.

SHORTER WALK

FROM the Junction Inn at Norbury (point 3) follow the main route through to point 5 which is the right turn between houses in Norbury village. Instead of taking this turning, however, continue on the lane which turns sharp right after about 300 yards and shortly after this you bear left at a junction to continue on the lane for about another half a mile back to the pub.

As mentioned in the main walk text you can trim the main walk a little if you wish by turning left on the lane from the Junction Inn up to point 5 and then pick up the main route again back to Forton Church. The length of this route is about 7¾ miles and could be called the Long Short walk or even the Short Long walk!

6
Ranton Priory

FACT*file*

MAPS: Landranger 127; Pathfinder 849 & 850

DISTANCES: 9½ miles; shorter walk 4½ miles

MAIN START: Any convenient place in Norbury Junction off the A519 Newport–Eccleshall Road. From Newport take a right turn about 1¼ miles after passing through Sutton but, if travelling from the opposite direction, the turning is left some 1½ miles after Woodseaves. You will firstly pass through Norbury and Norbury Junction is reached via lanes after a further mile. GR 793228. **Alternatively,** you could start the walk from Ranton Green (see below) and break at The Junction Inn at Norbury Junction. This walk does in fact link with walk 5 which has The Junction Inn as the featured pub but approaches it from the opposite direction.

    Public Transport: Nothing suitable.

SHORT START: The Hand and Cleaver at Ranton Green, which is tucked away in the maze of lanes to the west of Stafford and can be approached via the A518 and a right turn at Haughton, or from the B5405 and a left turn two miles south-west of Great Bridgeford. The pub is situated in an isolated spot on a junction about 1¼ miles south of Ranton Village but there are a few signs around to guide you. GR 846228.

    Public Transport: Nothing suitable.

TERRAIN: Easy walking over pleasant countryside taking in some attractive woodland, parkland and an eerie ruined priory. Some fields may be planted in summer but should be walkable at most times.

THE PUB: The Hand and Cleaver may be isolated but it certainly does not lack for custom. It is a handsome building dating from 1680 and has a comfortable interior which still retains some of its period atmosphere. A Bass free house serving a variety of ales including Caffreys, Highgate Dark, Worthington, Joules Crown and Guinness. Restaurant meals or bar snacks available. Beer garden. *Normal opening times.*

For details on the Junction Inn see walk 5.

FROM the bridge over the Shropshire Union Canal walk along the lane going in a south-easterly direction past the entrance to Norbury Junction Marina, which is a popular mooring and re-stocking place for narrow-boats. It is a hive of activity throughout the year and a wonderful place for just pottering about. After about 150 yards, as the lane starts to swing right, bear left along the concrete driveway to Norbury Manor. Shortly after the house you will go through a waymarked opening, passing by the remains of a moat on the left. The right of way is now across

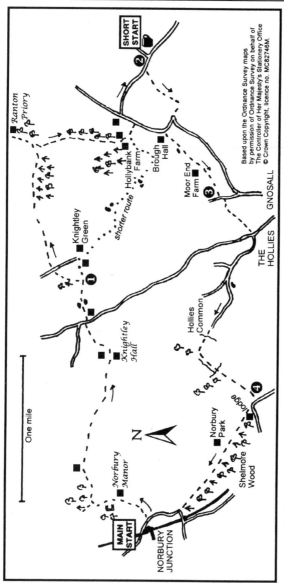

the facing field but it appears much more sensible to keep to the track and it does seem to be the intention that you should. Continue then on the concrete surface around the field as it loops to reach a fork at the corner of a wood.

Branch right here along the edge of the wood and keep going past farm buildings. Shortly afterwards, where the way swings left by a 'Private – No Right of Way' sign, continue directly ahead into a large field to the right of a boundary fence. If you are following the Pathfinder map you may observe that the wooded areas marked as 'Boggy Rough' and 'Big Champions' are no more! At the end of the field go through a gap in a crossing boundary beneath an oak tree then forward on a bearing very slightly right over the next field heading towards a lone tree on the far boundary. At times when this field is planted there is, hopefully, a path marked across it.

On reaching the boundary, go through a timber gate and ahead on a broad track with a post and wire fence on your right. Pass through a gateway in a crossing boundary and press onwards along a track which shortly loops right towards Knightly Hall (ignoring a cattle grid crossing on the right). Cross a cattle grid in front of farm buildings and proceed on the metalled track between them. At the end of the buildings the way sweeps left, crosses over another cattle grid and then bears right over a bridge before rising to cross yet another cattle grid and exit onto a lane.

Cross the lane diagonally right following the waymark on a telegraph pole to the left of a cottage onto a grassy track between hedgerows. Pass between two pools and through a metal gate into a field following the fence to the right hand pool for about 15 yards before continuing the line straight ahead across the field to another gate on the far boundary some 150 yards away. **❶**

Go through the gate and bear left following the ditched field edge passing a small plantation to exit via a gate to the right of a cottage to meet a crossing tarmac lane. Cross directly onto a waymarked bridleway, a broad stony track which continues for some distance. You will go through a gate into fields and through more gates to pass by a conifer plantation. This is a pleasant landscape and, if walking in May, the rhododendron flowers here are quite spectacular. The ruins of Ranton Priory are now in sight and you go through a gate 100 yards below it and turn left to get a closer view.

RANTON PRIORY. *The western tower is now all that remains of the twelfth century Saint Augustinian priory which fell victim to Henry VIII's policy of dissolution. Adjacent to it is the Abbey House, a huge building which was destroyed by fire during the second world war while in the occupation of Dutch soldiers. There is no public access, which is probably fair enough as the ruins are very dilapidated and these days are home for jackdaws only. The Earl of Lichfield is the present owner and a scheme has been mooted to restore the house to its original state – a rather expensive project I fear.*

Retrace your steps to the gate but go just beyond it to bear left across a waymarked stile. Follow the path to the left of a post and wire boundary,

The tower of Ranton Priory and the remains of the Abbey House

31

go through a further gate and continue on to another adjacent to a wood. If you look back from here you will get the best view available of the Priory. After negotiating this gate, carry on the track towards the left end of a large mixed tree plantation ahead. The next gate will lead you onto a stony track to Hollybank Farm and you go through another onto a concrete driveway between the buildings. On reaching a waymark post after the farm, continue forward for about 200 yards to gain access onto a lane. Turn left here and then right after another 150 yards or so and follow this lane for around half a mile to arrive at the Hand and Cleaver. **❷**

The Hand and Cleaver, Ranton Green

Try to avoid settling in for a prolonged stay in this comfortable pub and, having persuaded yourself to leave, turn right along the approach lane. After 200 yards look for a stile in the hedge on your left. Cross this onto a narrow, winding path through trees, parts of which can get overgrown at times. Cross a further stile and then two more on each side of a track to bear slightly left across a field to reach another stile in a crossing boundary about 150 yards ahead. If the field is planted it is easy to follow the edge around to the same point. Cross this and the next field aiming for two trees on the opposite boundary, where there is a further stile at a crossroads of paths. DO NOT CROSS THIS STILE, instead turn 90 degrees right in front of it along the adjacent edge of the field to exit via a stile onto a lane.

Turn right on the lane to arrive at Brough Hall after about 150 yards. As the lane swings right just before the buildings, there is a waymarked gate on your left. Go through into a field following the right boundary and, where this kinks right, continue directly forward across the side of the field to the top right corner. Close to the corner is a stile to cross before bearing right with the hedged boundary, which very quickly turns sharply left. You will shortly pass a pool on your right in a hollow and have Moor End Farm visible ahead right.

At the end of the field go though a gate and continue your line forward but now with the boundary on your left. On reaching the end of this next field, go through the second gateway on your left and proceed forward on the same line but with the boundary on your right again. Cross another stile and then a footbridge and stile to exit onto a narrow lane. ❸

Turn left and then right after 50 yards over a stile by a gate into a field, following the right boundary and with the village of Gnosall in view over to the left. Negotiate another stile in a crossing boundary after some 60 yards and bear left in the next field. You will pass through a gap in another crossing boundary and, at the end, go over another stile in front of a cottage and onto a lane. Turn right, then immediately left up a lane signed Hollies Common and No Through Road. The lane swings right past Hollies House and continues on through the agricultural community of The Hollies.

Keep left at a fork after which the lane dips past a red brick renovated cottage on the right, then rises again. You reach a fork at the top of the rise and here take the left option going gently downhill past Timbersbrook Cottage and through the hamlet of Hollies Common. Where the tarmac ends, continue forward along a grassy track which quickly narrows between hedges. Cross a footbridge and stile and a short field to another stile after 50 yards. Once over this continue in the next field along its left boundary and, at the end, cross a rickety fence stile and continue your line but now with boundary on your right.

You will soon be joined by a little brook and after about 150 yards go through a timber gate on your right to cross a small paddock before going through two more gates with a footbridge between them. Bear slightly left over the ensuing field towards the left side of a wood ahead, where there is a stile. Cross and climb along the left side of the trees to go over another stile. Now continue the line forward in a field passing between two tree-encircled hollows to a stile on the far boundary. Cross this and continue forward following a line of oak trees, then cross a further stile in the far boundary into another field with a hedge on your left. At the end cross what you might be relieved to know is the last stile, onto a lane and turn right. ❹

The lane swings left after about 100 yards and, at this point, continue forward on a tarmac driveway following the waymark to the right of Shelmore Lodge. The surface shortly turns to concrete and takes you along the edge of Shelmore Wood, through a most attractive corner between mature woodland and open countryside. Where the driveway veers right to Norbury Park Farm, continue ahead on the unmade track for perhaps another two thirds of a mile to reach a junction with a lane. Turn right here and follow the lane round for a third of a mile to arrive back at Norbury Junction.

SHORTER WALK

THE first section of the walk, until you join the long route at point (1), can be a little tricky with possible obstructions and cropped fields. This should not be a problem if you enjoy a challenge and take some secateurs but if these things bother you perhaps it would be better to give this one a miss.

With your back to the Hand and Cleaver turn right along the lane for about half a mile to reach a junction. Bear left here and after a further 200 yards branch right down the driveway to Hollybank Farm. Shortly before reaching the farm you will arrive at a crossroads of paths with a waymark post on the right and take what is perhaps the least obvious option to the left along the left side of a brick outbuilding. The path around the building could be overgrown (if it is you may have to go round the other side) and at the rear is a stile. Cross this and go left into a field with a hedge on your left and at the very top corner where hedgerows meet cross another, rather awkward, stile possibly obstructed with hedge.

Bear left now to cross a further stile in a hedge 30 yards ahead and continue in the next field with Brough Hall over to your left. Halfway along the field edge where the boundary fence kinks left, look for a waymark directing you 90 degrees right across the centre of the field towards a wood ahead. The field may be planted at times and, if so, there is little alternative but to walk through it. On reaching the trees, turn right to skirt round the edge of them with some pools below on your left. After the pools the path curves right to reach a stile in the hedge on your left after 50 yards – cross this and turn left along the field edge and follow it as it wiggles around for about 70 yards to find another stile in the hedge on your left.

Cross the stile and continue the same line but now with the hedge on your right (the waymark on the stile appears to give a misleading direction!). At the end of this long field you arrive at a gateway into the next field alongside a copse with another sunken pool. The right of way is through the gate and across the field passing to the right of a small tree-edged pool to exit via a gate in the opposite boundary to the left of an oak tree. If the field is planted you may find it necessary to consider walking around the edge. Turn right onto a broad track towards Knightley Green Farm.

As the track comes out of a 90 degree left turn cross a stile on your right and the footbridge beyond it into a field and cross the field cutting off the left side to reach the top left corner where there is a stile in front of a barn. Cross and turn right on a track up to the farm and follow it as it twists left then right between the buildings and turn left along another track running down to the right of the farmhouse. A distance of about 50 yards will bring you to a stile on your right which you cross into a field and follow the left hedged boundary to reach a small gate at the far end. This is point (1) on the long walk. DO NOT GO THROUGH THE GATE but turn right in front of it to follow the ditched field edge and the main walk to Ranton Priory and back to the Hand and Cleaver, point (2).

7
Stiperstones to Hope

FACT*file*

MAPS: Landranger 126; Pathfinder 888

DISTANCES: 7 miles; shorter walks 3, 3¼ or 4¼ miles

MAIN START: Anywhere convenient in the village of Stiperstones, situated about 10 miles south-west of Shrewsbury off the A488 Bishops Castle road. The best approach from the north is via a left turn at Ploxgreen and along the lane through Snailbeach or from the south via a right turn through Shelve. GR364005

Public Transport: Spasmodic service only (552) on schooldays and Saturdays but should be possible to plan a trip if you check the times carefully. *If walking on a weekday please bear in mind that The Stables Inn at Hopesgate is closed at lunchtimes (see below) and you could start from an alternative location to incorporate a break at the Stiperstones Inn.*

SHORT START: There is a choice of two short walks from Stiperstones and one from Hope/Hopesgate. The Stables Inn at Hopesgate is located three-quarters of a mile to the north of Hope, which is on the A488 four miles south of Minsterley. GR 343019.

Public Transport: As above. There is nothing to Hopesgate but the 552 also stops at Hope and you could easily start from there.

TERRAIN: Superb hill walking to start with magnificent views, followed by a descent into the gentler Hope Valley and return through woods and farmland. Walk at any time except when there is bad weather about. Some fairly stiff climbing is involved so do not attempt unless you are reasonably fit.

THE PUBS: The Stiperstones Inn has an olde-worlde charm, indeed it is about 300 years old, and is well frequented by walkers. There is a bar and lounge serving Boddingtons, Woods, Whitbread, Strongbow, Heineken and others. Excellent bar food available. Beer Garden. *Open every day from 11am to 11pm. If you can't make it home you can stay bed & breakfast.*

The Stables Inn also has a quaint olde-worlde character with beamed ceilings and stone fireplace. Ales on offer include Worthington, Tetleys, Robinsons, Guinness and Carlsberg plus Addlestones cider. Bar snacks and a selection of mouthwatering meals available. *Closed at lunchtimes during the week.*

STIPERSTONES. *The area around Stiperstones is a fascinating blend of majestic crags, folklore and ancient mines. It is dominated by the brooding quartzite ridge with its strangely shaped rocky outcrops thrusting dramatically skywards, which reach a peak with Manstone Rock some 1750 ft above sea level. Tales of the devil are rife as indeed are legends surrounding Wild Edric, an Anglo-Saxon character, after*

whom a long distance path over the South Shropshire hills is named.
It is said that if Wild Edric is seen galloping furiously over the hills it
is a portent of war. As for ancient mines, the locality is peppered with
old lead mines, once the most productive in Europe. They can be seen
best at Snailbeach, Shelve and Gravels. The latter boasts the oldest of
these reputed to date back to Roman times. The Stiperstones Inn was
a former mineworkers alehouse (not the Roman ones though!). Lots
to explore when you have time.

WITH your back to the Stiperstones Inn turn right and after a few
yards right again by a telephone kiosk taking the right fork along
a waymarked bridleway signed Perkins Beach Dingle. This loops
to the right to climb past a converted chapel and about 15 yards after that bear left up a concreted driveway. You go across the front of two cottages and , on reaching a third cottage, divert left down a grassy track, through two gates some 80 yards apart then continue on a narrower track between ash trees.

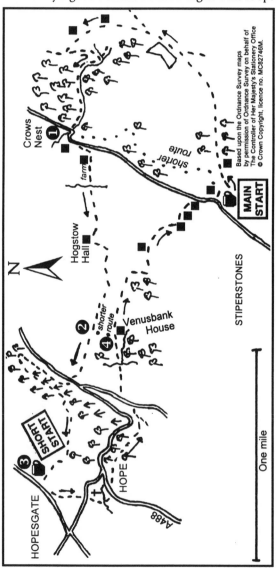

The track shortly opens out into a paddock in front of an isolated cottage and you cross it diagonally to go though a gate onto a broad grassy track between trees. It will not be long before you come to an information board about the Stiperstones and one of its legends about the Devil. We will take in the extreme northern end of the range on this walk but the main ridge can be seen at various points on the route.

If you look around you will notice that you are in a huge 'bowl' surrounded on all sides by ridges and I'm afraid a strenuous climb will be required to get out of it. I can promise you, however that the effort will be worthwhile. Continue ahead and uphill on the grassy track which narrows and becomes much steeper towards the top of the ridge. Take care as getting a good foothold can be a little difficult in places particularly in damp weather. When you get to the top the view backwards is spectacular with the village of Stiperstones below and the gentler hills beyond which are your eventual destination.

On reaching level ground continue on the track directly forward as views open up to the left towards Minsterley. The track broadens out and passes to the right of some trees bordering a fenced off enclosure. About halfway between the end of the enclosure and a hedge line some 150 yards ahead, leave the broad track in favour of a narrower one to the left. You pick up a fence on your right and stay ahead with a wooded valley below on the left before crossing a stile to proceed on a grassy track through bracken. Ignore a small gate on your right and stay on the track as it bears round to the left and passes by some corrugated metal buildings then another after a further 150 yards. Another 150 yards or so will bring you to a waymark post where you turn sharp left downhill on a narrow path.

The path twists and winds and eventually brings you to a small stream crossing. However, do not cross the stream but turn right in front of it to continue the descent with the stream on your left. After a few yards bear right onto a broader crossing track to maintain the downward momentum now with another stream on your left. This is an attractive path through deciduous woodland and you stay on it through an area of cottages and

Looking back to the Stiperstones

smallholdings to reach a junction with a lane in a settlement with the intriguing name of Crowsnest. ❶

Turn left on the lane and round an S-bend before passing an unusual residence on your right converted from an old engine house. Just after the property branch right along a waymarked bridleway on the entrance drive to Central Farm. Ignore a stile immediately on the right and stay on the broad track until immediately after passing the farm buildings where you go right at a waymarked junction. You will pass through three gates and come out into a field where you follow the right boundary. After going through another gate you enter onto an enclosed track, cross a brook and go through a further two gates to walk along an avenue of trees.

The track loops right to Hogstow Hall and you go though another two gates along the rear of the property after which you follow the track 90 degrees left to arrive at the next gate in front of an open field. Once through bear right along the field edge and after about 120 yards, at the end of the field, you go through another gate with a notice posted on it forbidding you to gallop. Please take note – I don't want to hear of any users of this book getting into trouble for not obeying instructions! Keep ahead with a fence on your left before going through a further gate to continue on a broad straight track between fences. At the end you go through yet another gate to reach a junction with a concreted lane. ❷

Bear right, although effectively continue ahead, on the lane and go through some more gates to exit onto the A488. Turn left on the main road then branch off right after only 25 yards into Hope Valley Nature Reserve. There is an Information Board at the entrance which you pass before entering a narrow track up the side of a wooded escarpment. The track can get boggy in parts as you walk above and to the rear of some property fronting the main road and, shortly after that, you bear left at a fork to reach a waymark at the top of the incline which directs you left along the top edge of the wood. After a while you pass a waymark post on your left and after another 300 yards, just past another waymark, you will find a stile in the fence on your right which takes you out of the wood into a large pasture field.

Take care over direction here. You need to keep right but move away from the boundary on your right towards a crossing boundary which you may not immediately be able to see. Do not be tempted to veer left uphill towards the tree line. Hidden in trees in the crossing boundary there is a stile – cross and follow the tree line on the left for a few yards then strike ahead on the same line across a pasture field. After about 80 yards look over to your right for a stile in the right field boundary a similar distance away and turn to make for that. Cross the stile and a little footbridge and bear slightly left heading to the left of a white painted building ahead and into the field corner. Here there is another stile to cross before turning right onto a lane to arrive at the white painted building which is in fact The Stables Inn. ❸

You may be relieved to learn that you have completed the most taxing part of the walk but do not sink into such a state of lethargy that further progress becomes impossible. On leaving re-cross the last outward stile and turn right to walk alongside the right hedge then tree boundary. At the end of the field cross another stile and continue forward on the same line to the left of a boundary fence and, as this kinks right, continue ahead across the field for 50 yards to a stile in the far boundary which exits onto a lane.

Turn right then immediately left down a waymarked path between hedgerows which runs around the rear of Hope church (locked at the time of my visit) and takes you through a small metal gate, after which keep left at a fork to cross a footbridge. Proceed on a path between timber fencing to exit onto the main road again.

Turn left along footpath in front of the church but cross the road carefully after 30 yards to go over a stile into a field. Keep to the right boundary and shortly cross another stile to continue the line forward over a scrubby field. You will be obliged to get through some overgrown hedging into the next field where you proceed with the tree boundary on your right.

The way twists around to reach a waymarked timber gate, around which the ground may be muddy, and you go through into deciduous woodland. Cross a stile after which there is wood on the left and field on the right, ignore another stile on your right and continue ahead with a fence line to reach another stile in the middle of nowhere! No need to cross it so stay with the fence on a descent to cross a footbridge onto a shaled track.

At this point you can see the Stiperstones crags directly ahead. Turn left on the shaled track and left again after 150 yards at a junction with a tarmac lane. After a further 100 yards or so you come to a crossing right of way and branch off right over a stile into a field. Keep to the right hedged boundary until at the bottom of the field you are diverted left then

The Stables Inn, Hopesgate

immediately right down an embankment to a footbridge in some trees. Go over it and proceed directly forward for about 50 yards to cross another stile to the left of a hollow.

Stay ahead now on a track above the hollow, which has a brook running through it, and emerge from the trees to find yourself in a scrubby field with buildings ahead. As you aim towards the left of them you will find it necessary to climb up an embankment on your left to reach level ground and the next stile. Cross this and the next a few yards further on to exit onto a shale track. ❹

The exquisite black and white Venusbank House is off to your right but do not take either of the shaled tracks leading in its direction but enter the concreted driveway more or less directly ahead, signed Venusbank Farm. The next section is a little complicated to explain. As the track veers round to the right towards the farm outbuildings continue straight ahead over a fence stile to the right of a metal gate onto a track between fence and hedge. At a point where the track narrows between fencing leave this route through a gate on your right to continue the same line to the right of the fence.

Where the enclosed track you were previously following ends in a gate bear half right across a scrubby area of small fir trees to a metal gate in the opposite hedge line. Go through this and veer immediately left on a grassy track to climb gradually with a hedge on your left and fence on your right. Continue through a gate and as soon as the ground starts to fall take the yellow waymark taped gate in the right fence into a long narrow field at the base of a wooded hill. I hope all these things are still in place now!

Keep to the left boundary and, after about 150 yards, a waymark post directs you left over a stile into the adjacent field in which you proceed downhill heading towards farm buildings. You will find a gate close to the bottom left corner of the field and to the right of the buildings. Go through and cross a farm track, through a wicket gate to the right of buildings into a paddock and then walk across the paddock to another wicket gate in the bottom boundary 60 yards ahead.

Once in the next field follow the left hedged boundary to a stile after 100 yards which you cross into a small open field and bear slightly right across it to another stile in the far boundary. Once over veer half right to go through a gate which exits onto a track in front of a brick and timber renovated cottage. Now turn left onto the broad earth track which takes you over a cattle grid to pass in front of some houses and exits onto a lane where you turn right back into Stiperstones.

SHORTER ROUTES

From Stiperstones

1. Distance 3¼ miles

FOLLOW the main walk from the start to point 1 and the junction with the lane at Crowsnest. Turn left on the lane through an S-bend to pass an unusual dwelling converted from an old engine house. You can now simply continue on the lane for two-thirds of a mile or so back into Stiperstones but, for a rather more interesting alternative, just after this point take the waymarked stile opposite in the left hedge and proceed ahead on a gently rising farm track. You cross a cattle grid where you are confronted with a gate clearly labelled 'No Right of Way'. Here you double back on a grassy waymarked track to ascend a hill for about 15 yards before going through another hairpin to continue the climb.

Go through a waymarked gate to pass directly in front of whitewashed stone cottages and continue ahead to exit cottage garden via a further waymarked gate. You now enter the Stiperstones Nature Reserve again and stay ahead on a grassy track with a post and wire fence on the right. Where the fence veers right follow the waymark direction half right along a path through bracken to enter a deciduous wood and contine the gentle ascent on an indistinct path. You soon meet the woodland boundary on your right and follow this as it first rises then sharply drops and turns hard left.

The path continues along the edge of the wood and eventually emerges into an area of bracken and heather with wonderful views opening out to the right. Proceed along the path keeping to a post and wire boundary on your right as it gently rises and falls. Eventually it descends steeply for about 20 yards (can be slippy, so take care) to meet a stone crossing track. Turn right and immediately cross a waymarked stile alongside a metal gate to enter a bus garage area. Go down to the left of the garage and a subsequent house to emerge onto a lane in Stiperstones and turn left back to the start.

2. Distance : 4¼ miles

FROM the starting point follow the main route through to point 2 and the junction with a concreted lane. Here turn left for about 150 yards to arrive at a junction of tracks in front of Venusbank House, which is point 4. Turn left again now up the concreted track and pick up the main route from point 4 back to Stiperstones.

From Hope/Hopesgate

Distance: 3 miles

PICK up the main route from your starting point and follow it through to point 4 and the stile which exits onto a shale track by Venusbank House. Turn left on the track going away from the house. After 150 yards it turns to concrete at point 2 and here bear left to continue with the main route again back to the start.

8
Much Wenlock

FACT*file*

MAPS: Landranger 126,127,136 & 137; Pathfinder 889,890,910 & 911 (sorry – it had to happen sometime!)

DISTANCES: 8¼ miles; shorter walk 3 miles

MAIN START: The village of Harley, which is located just off the A458 about 2½ miles out of Much Wenlock towards Shrewsbury. Limited roadside or verge parking. GR 595015

> **Public Transport:** Bus service 436/437 Bridgnorth/Shrewsbury stops at Harley Church. Also limited service 861 (Tues and Thurs) from Much Wenlock.

SHORT START: The George and Dragon in the centre of Much Wenlock (High Street) GR 623998

> **Public Transport:** As above. Service 436/437 also stops in Much Wenlock.

TERRAIN: Varied with loads of interest, taking in part of Wenlock Edge with some spectacular views, the historic town of Much Wenlock and pleasant woods and farmland. There are a number of climbs and two of them are quite stiff. Walk at any time of year.

THE PUB: The George and Dragon is a unique experience – like walking into the middle of the last century with Victorian artefacts and memorabilia adorning every wall and surface, as well as the largest collection of whisky water jugs you have ever seen, reputedly the largest in the country in fact. It is also a paradise for real ale enthusiasts boasting a number of temptingly sounding brews such as Dorothy Goodbody and Hook Norton. Bar snacks available or eat more grandly in the superb restaurant (as you may have guessed I rather like this place – it has a great atmosphere!).

Normal opening times

HARLEY. *Easily missed if you are travelling on the A458 which sweeps by to the east of the village and leaves it in splendid isolation in the shadow of Wenlock Edge. Harley Bank, from which there are some magnificent views, takes the A458 through a limestone cutting which was said to have been formed by French prisoners during the Napoleonic wars. The village accommodates a huge range of different properties from the expensively picturesque to modern and even totally neglected, all of which lends it a pleasant charm. The church is the focal point but unfortunately is kept locked – a sad indictment of current times. Some Roman antiquities have been discovered which has heightened speculation that Harley was situated on an important route, perhaps linking with the A5.*

TAKE the lane opposite the church signed Downes and Rowley. This is a 'No Through Road' and, whilst it is necessary to stay on it for about one and a half miles, I don't think you will find that a chore at all. You will pass through a residential area then descend past 'Castle Hill' on the left, a large early Victorian property. The lane levels out and swings through an S-bend before crossing a bridge and continuing with the escarpment of Wenlock Edge coming ever closer.

Eventually, you arrive at a T-junction with Rowley Farm some way over to the right. However, the way is left in front of Rowley Cottage to reach a gateway immediately beyond it leading into a field. Although the definitive route crosses the field diagonally, local walkers use the much more practical permissive path along the right edge of the field which proceeds on a rising course to exit at the top onto a broad crossing track. ❶

Turn right here past Blakeway Cottage and just before reaching Blakeway Farm after another 250 yards, bear left through a gate onto a track which rises between trees to bring you out into a clearing. Turn left at this point across the clearing and through a swing gate onto a narrower path leading along the bottom of the Edge. After about a quarter of a mile you will reach a point where the trees on the left thicken and here you

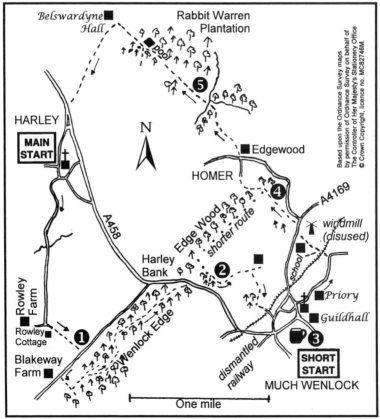

43

need to branch off to the right – but read the following directions carefully as the correct course is not immediately obvious.

On your left is a wicket gate leading into a field – ignore that, it is just a landmark so that you know you are in the right place! There is a faint path off to the left and the main path continues ahead uphill. You don't take that either, or at least only for about 10 yards before scrambling up the embankment on your right to turn left onto a narrow path which also goes uphill (and is not clearly visible from the lower level) at an angle of about 30 degrees to the main path. O.K., I have done my best to put you on the right track and you will soon know if you *are* right as a fairly stiff climb will bring you to a waymark post at a much broader crossing track where you turn left onto the Jack Mytton Way (see the Long Mynd walk (11) for a note on 'Mad Jack'). Continue on this until you arrive at a gate. Go through for a few yards to a junction of tracks at the National Trust sign and bear left downhill following the waymark to Harley Bank.

There are some good views from this path over Harley Bank towards the Severn Valley although they are restricted to glimpses through the trees. Part way down the slope you fork right on a path which again leads upwards and can be muddy at times. Ignore a fork right on reaching more level ground and stay on the main track signed Harley Bank. Continue ahead at junction with a broader track coming in from the left and at the top of the rise go forward through a waymarked gate after 200 yards to exit onto the main road after a further 100 yards. Turn right and proceed carefully along the main road for about 100 yards before branching off left through a waymarked gate and onto a broad track between pine trees. At the end of the wood you reach a junction of paths with the shorter route coming in from the left. ❷

Bear right into a field following the hedged right boundary which curves left and continues along the bottom edge of the same field. Go through a gap in a crossing boundary and continue towards a cottage in view ahead. At the end of this next field is a choice of routes – take the right option through a metal gate into the adjacent field to walk along the left hedged boundary heading towards the left side of a small wood. (Jack Mytton Way again) At the end of the field the path weaves into the wood and, on exiting, bear left onto a broad track down towards Much Wenlock.

On reaching a tarmac surface go straight ahead over a bridge, past an agricultural yard and, on reaching a junction with a road bear left. After 120 yards turn right following the sign to Wenlock Priory and at another junction bear right then right again in front of the Guildhall to arrive at the George and Dragon. ❸

MUCH WENLOCK. *There is so much to see in this fascinating town that it is impossible to encapsulate it in one short paragraph. The highlight, of course, is the hugely atmospheric ruined Priory which is now in the care of English Heritage but there are many more wonderful places to visit, not the least of which is the sixteenth century Guildhall. This is built partially over a medieval prison and until recently was used as a courtroom. Take a look at the plaque on the side wall which provides a guided tour around the town's places of interest or visit the Tourist Information Office at the Museum, a short distance from the George and Dragon. Whatever, try not to leave without soaking up some of the history which simply oozes from every ancient corner.*

When you do make the break, turn right then left past the Guildhall again but after passing Holy Trinity church bear right into Bull Ring towards the Priory ruins. Continue past the ruins on a quiet lane for about a third of a mile until you reach a crossroads where the metalled surface swings sharp right. Here bear left following a waymark and shortly descend via steps onto a dismantled railway line, a former branch of the GWR running between Wellington and Craven Arms. Cross it diagonally up more steps opposite and at the top is a complex junction of paths. Continue ahead on a virtual straight line on the second path from the left. There is a quarry spoil heap to the right and after a few yards you turn right at a junction onto the Jack Mytton Way again.

This path takes you along the rear of a school and exits via a gate onto the A4169. You may have spotted a ruined windmill on the rise to your right which you can visit although there is not a great deal to see. Turn right along the main road – there is a footpath – and after about 80 yards cross carefully to go left through a waymarked gate into a field.

Cross the field directly, keeping parallel with a wood on your left and go over a stile in a crossing boundary to continue forward to the left of a hedge. There are good views of the Wrekin over to the right from here and you can also see the cooling towers of Ironbridge Power Station. At a break in the hedge line curve left then right on a well defined path to pick up the hedge again, but now to the right of it and stay on line until reaching the front end of Edge Wood, the extreme north-eastern end of Wenlock Edge. Cross a stile into the wood. **❹**

WENLOCK EDGE. *Formed about 420 million years ago during the Silurian Period in a tropical sea, Wenlock Edge stretches in an unbroken line for 15 miles between Benthall Edge above the Severn Gorge to Craven Arms. The underlying rock is limestone built up from the skeletons and shells of sea creatures and subsequent earth movements created its present shape, tilting the rock strata gently down to the south-east. The limestone has been a valuable resource for building stone and as a flux in iron smelting. Even today it is quarried for aggregate along the edge of Blakeway Coppice. A substantial part is owned by the National Trust whose policy is to preserve the woodland cover yet increase public access by improved waymarking and the explorer will be rewarded with some excellent views, most notably at Major's Leap and Ippikin's Rock.*

Those on the short route will bear immediately left but you should take the right hand path descending steeply into the wood. Please take particular care along this section, which can be slippery in wet conditions. You exit via a stile and proceed leftwards across the top of a field along a descending

Homer from Wenlock Edge. The Wrekin is in the background.

ridge with splendid views of Homer village below. The way loops left through a gap in a crossing tree line after which you turn right to walk along the left side of the same tree line to a stile by a gate in front of a bungalow. Cross onto a track between hedgerows and cross another stile out onto a tarmac lane. Proceed ahead on the lane, ignoring the turning left, through an attractive residential area to arrive at a T-junction.

Cross directly over a stile at the side of the drive to 'Edgewood' onto a grassy track alongside the garage. This leads shortly to another stile which you cross into a field and, after about 80 yards, cross a further stile and continue in the next field following the left boundary. There are further good views of the Wrekin here over to the right. Cross another stile after which the boundary kinks left but you continue ahead following the waymark direction more or less parallel with the left tree line as it dips then loops left to a footbridge on the left in a valley bottom. **❺**

Cross the footbridge (*do not be tempted by the stile off to the right*) before striking forward up quite a steep field towards a hedged ridge. You may be able to spot a stile in a fenced gap in the hedge and when you reach it you will find there are some fairly steep steps up to it. Cross into the next field and go directly forward aiming to the right of a small wood ahead. Go along the side of the trees and where they end proceed through a gate and cross the ensuing field, cutting off the right corner of it and aiming towards the end of a fence line in front of a larger wood coming in from the right. This is Rabbit Warren Plantation and you should find a gate leading into it on a broad track. After literally only 10 yards fork left down a grassy track between trees, which can get muddy at times.

You will arrive at a small lake and bear round to the left of it over what again can be boggy ground to exit via a stile onto a broad track. Turn right here and stay on the track for about a third of a mile to meet a crossing track in front of Belswardyne Hall. Turn left through a gate alongside the walled boundary to the Hall and then go through another gate at the end of the wall. Now continue on a broad farm track as it snakes through pleasant countryside with views over Wenlock Edge. After crossing an open field continue forward across the next to the right of a boundary hedge to eventually exit via a gate onto the A458. Turn left on the wide grass verge and cross the road after about 120 yards before turning right down the lane back into Harley.

SHORTER WALK

FROM the George and Dragon, point 3, follow the long route to point 4 and cross the stile into the wood. Those on the long walk will take the path to the right downhill but you should climb the short embankment to follow the path to the left of the wood. The path rises to a boundary where there is a gap to go through before continuing ahead and through another gap in the next crossing boundary. Stay on course along the wood edge and go through a further hedge boundary (ignoring a waymarked path on the left) and the next to yet another where there is a waymarked stump on the right at a convergence of paths.

At this point turn left to follow the right hand side of the hedge heading towards the left of a small wood. Enter the wood keeping the same line and after a short distance you pass a broad track on the right where the main route comes in (point 2). After this point transfer to the left side of the field boundary hedge and rejoin the main route text back to the start.

9
Picklescott

FACT*file*

MAPS: Landranger 126 & 137; Pathfinder 889 & 910

DISTANCES: 8¾ miles; shorter walk 3½ miles

MAIN START: On or around the green by the church in Church Pulverbatch, about eight miles south-west of Shrewsbury City Centre. Unless you are familiar with the area the best approach from Shrewsbury may be via the A488 through Hanwood, turning left down to Longden and on to Church Pulverbatch. Don't get confused between Church Pulverbatch and Castle Pulverbatch which is located half a mile to the south. GR 429029

   Public Transport: Bus service 546 from Shrewsbury stops in Castle Pulverbatch. However, the walk can easily be started from there.

SHORT START: The Bottle & Glass in Picklescott, about four miles to the south of Church Pulverbatch and approached via the lanes from that direction or east from the A49 Shrewsbury-Church Stretton road. GR435994.

   Public Transport: nothing suitable.

TERRAIN: Superb hill country with pretty rural villages. Plenty of climbing although nothing really strenuous and some excellent viewpoints. Walk at any time.

THE PUB: Brilliant, idyllic and practically every other complimentary adjective you can think of! Charmingly situated in a quiet backwater, the Bottle & Glass has a wonderful olde-worlde character with low beamed ceilings, tiled floors and open fireplace. Serving Bass, Worthington and Guinness on draught. Bar snacks and a mouth-watering selection of meals in the restaurant. Outside seating. *Normal opening times.*

IF you have the time now or at the end of the walk the church of St. Editha is worth a visit. It still contains Victorian box pews and a gallery with a somewhat neglected air although a major restoration project underway at the time of research may by now have changed that. The tomb of Sukey Harley, whose story is told by J.H.Alexander in *More than a Notion* is located at the east end of the circular churchyard. For those few of you who did not already know, St. Editha was born in 962 and was a daughter of King Edgar.

On with the walk – from the parking place turn left to a junction then right towards Castle Pulverbatch with Broom Hill visible over on the right. On reaching a junction with a more major road bear left into Castle Pulverbatch.

You will pass two pubs close together, the Woodcock and the White

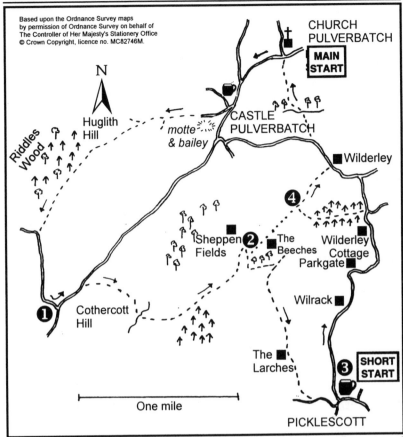

Horse, and shortly after the latter take the right fork along a lane signed Habberley, Minsterley and Pontesbury. Those entering the White Horse might be amused by a rhyme to be found there which goes 'Cothercott upon the Hill, Wilderley down in the dale, Churton for pretty girls and Pulverbatch for good ale'. It would be nice to have time to carry out a detailed study of these claims!

PULVERBATCH – *a little confusing to non-locals; Pulverbatch, Church Pulverbatch, Castle Pulverbatch! The village comprises a number of different segments including Cothercott and Wilderley, all of which you will pass by on the walk. Church Pulverbatch, known locally as Churton, is the proper parish name although Castle Pulverbatch contains the majority of the population and serves as the social centre with its pubs and shop. The prefix of 'Castle' derives from the fine motte & bailey which you will see shortly. It occupies a strategic defensive position and was one of many built by the Normans just after the Conquest to control the Marches. It was used as a look-out post in the last war by the Home Guard in case the Germans tried to invade from Wales. In the Middle Ages the village was an important stop for drovers from The Long Mynd.*

After a few yards the lane swings right towards those places but you continue ahead along a narrower tarmac lane. Just after the houses end you pass the motte & bailey on the left, which can be visited. Ignore a footpath opposite and keep ahead: after a while the tarmac changes to a broad track and you can see Lawn Hill on the right with Huglith Hill more or less straight in front. This area was at one time a hive of mining activity, mainly for copper and barytes. A mine at Huglith Hill used an aerial rope-way to transport materials for processing at Malehurst. Now farming is the principal industry.

Ignore all paths off and you should shortly be able to see the hills around Cothercott over to your left, visibility permitting. The track continues past Riddles Wood and just through the trees you can see a large depression in the ground marking the location of a former mine shaft. After this point Cothercott Hill comes into view on the half left and this is our immediate destination. Eventually you arrive at a junction with a tarmac lane and bear left along it for just under half a mile to meet the Shrewsbury road again.

❶

Turn left along the road as it rises gently, and after about a quarter of a mile look for a footpath sign and stile on your right. Cross the stile and bear half left through an area of gorse and continue the same bearing in a pasture field to pass to the right of some old mine workings. Aim now for the valley between two ridges and pick up a clear track through the gap where you will find a waymark sign on a fence post directing you forward to the right of a post and wire fence. The way loops right then descends into a valley with attractive rolling countryside all around. At the bottom cross a stile, then a brook (no footbridge) and a small patch of marsh grass to veer left following a waymark to continue with a post and wire fence on your left.

There now follows a steepish climb before the track levels out briefly, then descends towards a waymarked gate and fence stile to the left of a pine wood, where you will note that you are presently on the Shropshire Way. The waymark is slightly misleading as it guides you more to the right – the correct route is directly ahead across rough undulating ground to the right of a tree lined ditch. There are some minor obstacles such as marshy grass and gorse bushes to contend with but, at the bottom of the gentle downward slope, is a waymarked gate. Go through and ahead on the same line following a sparse tree boundary towards Sheppen Fields Farm. The route from here becomes a little illogical and not particularly precise. Carry on towards the farm until you are about 100 yards away from it, just after a kink in the boundary. Then strike sharp right, i.e. about 130 degrees, across the field to a stile which you can see on the opposite boundary (not the one in the top field corner which you may also be able to see). I say 'illogical' because it would have saved some distance to have taken a less acute right turn earlier to reach this point but these paths were created many years ago for reasons which are long since forgotten. ❷

Cross the stile and descend through a field following the right boundary and pass through a gateway at the bottom a few yards to the right of a small wood. Bear left here on a permissive path rising to the right of the wood but, as the wood ends, move gradually away from the left boundary across and up an undulating field – after a while you will see a waymark post ahead. Having reached the post, go through a gate in the field corner and turn right onto a broad farm track. Continue on this ignoring all paths off to the right to pass The Larches Farm, after which the track becomes metalled and descends before rising again to meet a junction with a lane. Bear left to enter the isolated rural community of Picklescott with its picturesque cottages and farms and turn left in the village centre to find the Bottle and Glass. ❸

PICKLESCOTT. *An isolated rural community with picturesque cottages and farms. Unfortunately, it has gone the way of so many similar villages and lost most of its former crafts and trades; in days gone by Picklescott supported a wheelwright, carpenter, blacksmith and an undertaker as well as another pub called The Gate Hangs Well. Oh well, I suppose some would call it progress! Anyway, the pub it has still got is super and delightfully situated alongside a stream which passes through the village.*

I have no doubt that the temptation to remain firmly rooted to your seat will prove almost irresistible, particularly if the day is fine and you can sit outside and watch the world (and the ducks) go by. When you do manage to break away, turn right up the lane past Hall Farm and the entrance to Pogan Hall. After another a quarter of a mile along this pleasant lane you will pass Wilrack Farm on the left, after which expansive views open up over countryside to the north. Continue on past Parkgate where the lane swings right and after another a quarter of a mile bends left between a

The Bottle and Glass, Picklescott

couple of cottages. Wilderley Cottage appears next and shortly afterwards you reach a turning on the right.

You can short cut the walk by continuing ahead along the lane for another half a mile into Wilderley but a much more attractive option is to branch left opposite the right turn referred to along a waymarked bridleway into a pine wood. There may be a few home made horse jumps to negotiate as the path winds an attractive course for about a third of a mile to exit from the wood via a stile into a field. Keep to the left boundary for about 50 yards before cutting half right up through the field towards a ramshackle metal barn which is partly obscured by the brow of the rise at first. To the left of the barn is a waymarked gate in front of a junction with the Shropshire Way. **4**

Turn right and enter onto a broad grassy wedge of land between fences, go through a waymarked gate and continue on a narrower track which soon broadens out again at Wilderley Farm. Turn left onto a lane and after about 300 yards, just as it begins to climb slightly, fork right up a broad farm track, which shortly turns into a green lane between high hedges. After a while this descends to cross a ford via a footbridge and then continues upwards before levelling out to bring you back to Church Pulverbatch.

SHORTER WALK

STARTING from the Bottle and Glass, point 3, take the main route through to point 4 and the junction with the Shropshire Way. Those on the main walk will turn right here but you should bear left along the edge of a field bordering a fence and ditch. This is a long field and you follow the boundary to the end where there is a waymarked stile with Beeches Farm to your left and Sheppen Fields Farm to your right. Cross the stile and a track to go over another stile opposite to the left of a metal gate. After some 30 yards you come to a further stile on the left and have now arrived at point 2. Cross and now pick up the main route again back to the pub.

10
Astley Abbotts

FACT*file*

MAPS: Landranger 138; Pathfinder 911

DISTANCES: 8¼ miles; shorter walk 5 miles

MAIN START: On the lane near The Boldings farm to the north of Astley Abbotts, which itself is 2½ miles north of Bridgnorth off the B4373 Broseley Road. Go through the village and after about a mile you approach The Boldings on your right – there is a pull-in on the right some 400 yards before the farm and another about 200 yards on the left after it. GR 713974/717973

> **Public Transport:** Nothing suitable to the start although bus services 9/99 Bridgnorth/Telford stop at Nordley and you could start the walk from there.

SHORT START: The Pheasant at Linley Brook off the B4373 about 5 miles north of Bridgnorth. GR 682978

> **Public Transport:** As above.

TERRAIN: Easy walking with one or two short climbs. Pleasant countryside and a particularly attractive section along the River Severn. Some fields may be planted in summer, particularly on the latter section.

THE PUB: A must for all Real Ale enthusiasts! A small welcoming walkers type Free House with numerous intriguing ales on offer including Shepherd Neame Spitfire, Cottage Southern, Sarah Hughes Sedgley Surprise, Miles Tap Bitter and Wells Eagle Bitter to name but a few, but they are changing constantly. Bar snacks available. Outside seating.

Normal opening times.

FROM wherever you have parked find the entrance drive to The Boldings and about 20 yards to the east of it on the opposite side of the lane climb up a short embankment and cross a stile into a field.

Proceed across centre of the field towards a wood where you can see another stile at the corner of it and, after crossing, descend at an angle of 45 degrees on an indistinct path through the wood which meanders down to meet a broader crossing track. Here turn left on to an attractive way alongside a line of fir trees. A few yards after the track starts to descend bear right at the fork and at the bottom you will meet a wide crossing track. In fact, this is the old Severn Valley Railway Track which formerly linked Bridgnorth and Shrewsbury and which was closed in 1970. Mercifully, the southern route to Kidderminster was restored and, as everyone knows, is now a major tourist attraction. Go straight across over a stile bearing half left over a field to a waymark post at the top of the river-bank.

Turn left to stroll for about 1¼ miles in all along a most beautiful section of river-bank. Without doubt it is one of the most picturesque stretches of the Upper Severn, particularly on a fine summer's day, and for the best part of the way the most likely form of company is fishermen as the area is relatively inaccessible by car. Off to the right is a magnificent three storey building of castle-like appearance which was the former Apley Hall, built for Thomas Whitmore in 1811, more latterly a boy's school and now, sadly, empty. You will cross a couple of stiles and pass under Apley Bridge.

APLEY. *A fascinating corner with a long history associated with the industrial revolution and the coal industry which space, or the lack of it, will not permit me to present in any detail. Apley Park on the other side of the river was the estate of William Orme Foster, M.P. 'Squire of Apley' and you might see on the bridge, which was built in 1905, a notice advising persons other than his tenants and friends of the need to obtain his permission to cross. A journal of the time commented that 'some limit has been necessary to stop bulldog owners and mischievous revellers who here, as elsewhere, have done all they could to close such places to the public'. Not a lot changes does it? The bridge linked the estate with the railway and the forge nearby, all of which must have been a hive of activity their heyday.*

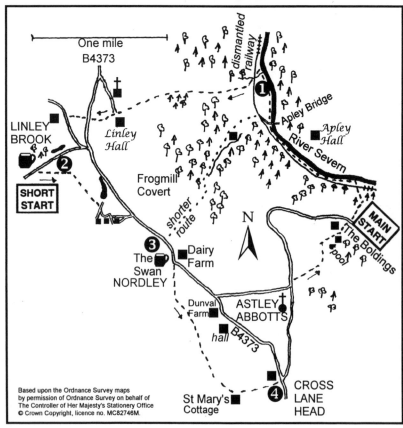

Cross a further stile on the other side of the bridge and keep on the riverbank and Severn Way. After another quarter of a mile or so you will reach a stile some 25 yards before a cottage. ❶

Having crossed the stile the official line is to proceed to the corner of the cottage garden and then, before crossing another stile, turn 135 degrees left alongside the outbuildings but this route is obviously unused. Instead turn immediately left after the first stile up a track to the left of the outbuildings and through a gateway onto the old railway line again. Turn left now but only for a few yards until crossing a bridge over a brook and,

Apley Bridge

immediately before a 'No Right of Way' sign, bear right down an embankment to a metal gate.

Go through and turn right to climb through undulating pasture keeping the tree boundary on your right (there is a dip before the ground starts to rise where it can get boggy). At the top you are funnelled onto a narrow track between trees before emerging into open ground. Carry on the climb to cross a stile by a gate giving access into another field and follow the left boundary as the ground begins to level out a little. You may feel inclined to pause for a while here to enjoy the view backwards over the wooded Severn Valley. The rate of ascent is much more gradual now as you follow the long field boundary and when it eventually flattens you can see the Wrekin diagonally to the right on a clear day.

Pass a mixed covert on the left and proceed on a broad stony track for about half a mile until it exits onto the B4373. Before reaching this point you will pass by Linley Hall and can take a short diversion along a track on the right to Linley church. A key can be obtained if you wish to look inside. Cross the main road directly and a field on the other side following the same line and the waymark direction. This field is frequently planted and, if so, you may find it easier to take the road alternative. Turn left on the B4373 for about a quarter of a mile, then branch right following a sign to The Pheasant. If crossing the field, head straight for the farm buildings in view and on the far side the land dips to reach an opening onto a quiet lane. Turn left along the lane for about a quarter of a mile and at a T-junction bear right to follow another lane through a residential area for a further quarter of a mile to arrive at The Pheasant. **②**

Having extracted yourself from the pub, turn right and continue along the lane for about 250 yards until coming across a cottage on the left bearing the number 70, just before the lane starts to descend. Here turn sharp left up a wide stone track which turns to grass after the last house and you reach what appears to be a dead end with gates to the front and left. Do not go through either of these, or into any of the adjacent fields, but look right and enter the narrow path leading between trees. This exits after about a third of a mile onto a broad stone crossing lane (beware – the path can get churned up in wet weather!).

Turn right then immediately left up a stone driveway, ignoring 'Private' sign, which takes you past two pretty cottages and, as the bend straightens out opposite the rear wall of the second cottage, bear left down a track between trees. This broadens out onto a stone driveway and passes by some further cottages before arriving at a T-junction. Turn left onto another driveway and keep on it until exiting onto the B 4373. It is now necessary to turn right along the road for about a third of a mile (take care as there is no footpath) to arrive at The Swan public house at Nordley. **③**

Those on the short route will leave the road at this point but, if following the main walk, continue on for a short distance through an S-bend by Dairy Farm and, right on the crown of the left bend, look for a waymarked stile into a field on your right partially obscured by a bend direction sign.

In the field keep to the right boundary and, at the end, bear left along the bottom hedged boundary. On walking down to this point on a clear day there are good views to the half right of Brown Clee with a glimpse of Titterstone Clee behind it together with a vista left over the wide expanse of countryside towards Bridgnorth.

At the end of the field cross stiles on each side of a track to enter the next field with Dunval Farm over to the left. The waymark directions on the second stile and a nearby stump may cause some confusion as they direct you 90 degrees right in front of the second stile into the adjacent field. *Carefully read the whole of the next paragraph before continuing further.*

Following the right of way you then bear left after some 50 yards through a metal gate and cross the next field (the one you would have gone into had you crossed the second stile) passing to the left of an oak tree to a second oak on the far boundary where there is another stile. *HOWEVER, when researching the route it seemed clear that you were intended to cross the second stile and then bear slightly right across the field to the next stile referred to – indeed the farmer had marked the way across, so presumably this is a permissive path.*

By whatever route you reach the stile by the oak, cross it and bear half right across the next (large) field, which again may be marked by the farmer when planted. Aim for the tree line ahead to the left of farm buildings further beyond in the distance. If the path is not marked it may be tricky to get the exact line but you should come across a double stile hidden in the tree line. Be careful as the first stile drops sharply on the far side and cross into another field following the left tree boundary.

At the end go through a gate in a crossing boundary and continue ahead in the next field. Go through a gap in another crossing boundary and continue the line to reach a gate in front of a house which leads you onto a broad track. The House is called 'St. Mary's Cottage' – some cottage! You pass in front of it and continue on the track for maybe a little over a quarter of a mile to exit on the B4373 again at Cross Lane Head. **4**

Cross the main road more or less directly and follow a lane to Astley Abbotts, a distance of about half a mile.

ASTLEY ABBOTTS. *A pretty village with an ancient history. It was mentioned in the Domesday Book as Estleia (East Lea) and came under the jurisdiction of Shrewsbury Abbey which is where the 'Abbotts' part of the name originated. The church is dedicated to St. Calixtus, an unusual name which begs an explanation. St. Calixtus was an Italian and a slave in Caesar's household and, to cut a long story short, he was made Bishop of Rome in 219 before being martyred by being put down a well during a riot. Why the church is dedicated to him is not clear. It was built in the twelfth century and almost entirely rebuilt during the reign of Charles I. The maidens glove and garland in the Nave are said to have belonged to a bride who was drowned on her wedding eve in 1707.*

On reaching the far side of the village, ignore the lane on your left but after a further 20 yards cross a somewhat dilapidated stile in the hedge on your right. Follow the field boundary, cross a further stile after 150 yards then a sleeper bridge and another stile. Continue in the next field still with the boundary on your right and cross a stile under an oak tree before bearing half right following a waymark for 20 yards until reaching a further oak tree. Here turn 90 degrees left with a tree boundary which, after another 50 yards, loops left to join a track running to the left of some fishing pools with The Boldings in view. Keep going until reaching the buildings, turn right in front of the farmhouse and then almost immediately left along a tarmac driveway which exits onto the lane and the start point.

SHORTER WALK

FROM The Pheasant, point 2, follow the long route through to The Swan at Nordley which is point 3. It may be as well that The Swan has very limited opening times and perhaps, therefore, it will not be necessary for you to resist the temptation to stop at two pubs within as many miles. Opposite the pub at the back of a small pull-in you will find a waymark post which takes you through a gate and along the right edge of a field. As you descend gently there are pleasant views over surrounding countryside and you go through another gate at the end into the next field following the fenced boundary which shortly changes to trees and arrive at a waymarked gate in front of Frogmill Covert.

Go through onto a narrow path in the covert for about 150 yards and exit via a gate to continue on the path as it winds around to the left of a clearing. The path can get muddy and becomes a little indistinct for a short while before meeting a broad track in front of a derelict cottage. Turn right here and shortly cross a footbridge to stay on the broad track. After another 200 yards or so at a fork keep directly ahead along a green lane bordering a brook, although you can bear left along the drier path as it comes out at the same place.

Keep going on this attractive path until about 100 yards after passing a cottage on your right you go through a gate giving access into a field. Follow the farm track which leads off half right through the pasture and then loops right to take you through a new timber gate and across a brook before climbing a short rise to meet a dismantled railway track. This is the former line of the old Severn Valley Railway linking Bridgnorth to Shrewsbury.

Cross the track diagonally to enter the lower of two paths facing you (i.e. the one further away from the cottage) and ignore the 'Private – authorised entry only' sign. This is a public Right of Way. You will shortly come to some cottages by Apley Bridge and take the waymarked path down to the left of it which leads down to the bank of the River Severn. There is some information on Apley in the main walk text although that route goes under the bridge whereas here you can see it from above.

Turn left along the river-bank and go over a stile. A distance of about a quarter of a mile will bring you to another stile with a cottage in view behind. This is point 1 on the main route and you simply follow the directions from there back to the start.

11
The Long Mynd

FACT*file*

MAPS: Landranger 137; Pathfinder 909 & 910

DISTANCES: 8¼ miles; shorter walk 4¼ miles

MAIN START: On the Long Mynd at 'Shooting Box' car park. From Church Stretton take the narrow, twisty road up the hillside that runs just to the south of Carding Mill Valley and, on reaching a fork after about two miles, bear right and the car park is on your right after another half mile. The same point can also be reached from the Bridges or Wentnor directions to the west. GR 422954

  Public Transport: None at all to the start point – bus/train to Church Stretton only.

SHORT START: The Crown Inn at Wentnor, a small village lying to the west of The Long Mynd and approached from the south via a turning off the A489 three miles east of Lydham or from the west along lanes off the A488. A local map would be useful. GR385928

  Public Transport: There is an infrequent service stopping at Wentnor but it is doubtful whether this would be practical.

TERRAIN: Spectacular hill walking along the top of one of the county's best known landmarks with a diversion into the pleasant low lying area to the west. Walk at any time of the year although inadvisable in the winter months if there is bad weather about.

THE PUB: A homely period pub with genial hosts, The Crown offers a comfortable yet 'local' atmosphere with a good range of ales. Wadsworth 6X, Old Speckled Hen. Boddingtons, Caffreys and Murphy's are usually available together with Heineken and Scrumpy Jack cider. As well as bar snacks, more substantial fare is served in the restaurant with a truly mouth-watering menu to tempt you. *Traditional opening times.*

THE LONG MYND *is probably the best known of the Shropshire Hills consisting of a large moorland plateau cut by a number of ravines running eastwards and called locally 'batches' or 'hollows'. It is superb walking country although parts are now so heavily visited that active measures to protect the environment are becoming increasingly important. The National Trust owns most of the Long Mynd and is constantly working to maintain the area's natural beauty for the benefit of all. However, it is still easy to escape into the vast acreage of this superb wilderness and, if you are a bird watcher, a large variety of upland birds will keep you absorbed for hours. The carpet of heather and bilberry (known locally as 'whinberry') provides ideal cover for grouse and The Mynd is in fact the most southerly grouse moor in Britain. Do enjoy this place of unique beauty but please also respect it and, of course, observe the usual precautions in uncertain weather conditions.*

TAKE the path opposite (The Jack Mytton Way) in a south westerly direction and, on reaching a broad crossing track, continue ahead to arrive at Pole Bank after a total distance of about three quarters of a mile. This is the highest point on the Long Mynd at 516m and there is a toposcope, built in 1986 to mark the diamond jubilee of the founding of the Council for the Protection of Rural England, which identifies the various landmarks visible from this superb vantage point. Incidentally, Jack Mytton was an eccentric Shropshire character who lived in the early part of the last century and known as 'Mad Jack'. Renowned for practical jokes

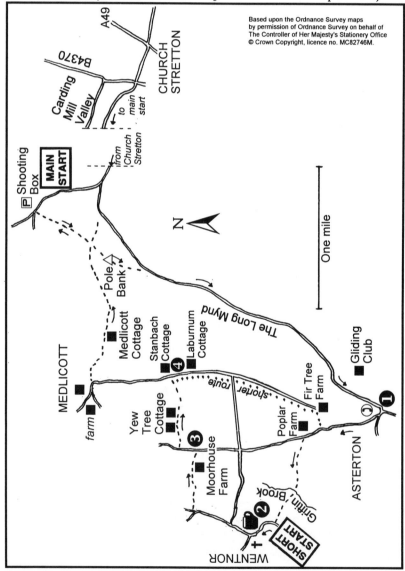

Based upon the Ordnance Survey maps by permission of Ordnance Survey on behalf of The Controller of Her Majesty's Stationery Office © Crown Copyright, licence no. MC82746M.

View from the Long Mynd

he turned to drink and got into debt, was put into debtors prison and died penniless in his late thirties.

Continue forward now with Corndon Hill and Heath Mynd clearly in view to the west and on reaching a junction with a tarmac lane turn right. You enter a long gradual descent then rise slightly before descending again to pass The Midland Gliding Club. The lane now starts to descend more steeply to pass a hang gliding club on the right with suberb views over Corndon Hill etc. As you go round a left bend there is a wonderful vista down into the valley on your right over farmhouses and patchwork quilt fields. Proceed on a steep descent towards the village of Asterton and, at the bottom, turn right at a junction by a phone box. ❶

Ignore a turning left to Wentnor after a few yards and walk through the small agricultural community with its attractive farmhouses. A distance of getting on for half a mile will bring you to Poplar Farm on the right and, immediately after here, go left through a gate and onto a waymarked path in a field. Follow the direction slicing off the left side towards the opposite boundary where there is a stile. Cross and continue in the next field alongside the left boundary and in the top left corner cross a further stile, turning right to go over another after 25 yards together with a footbridge over Griftin Brook.

Once in a field on the far side continue directly forward up the rise, ignoring a stile off to your left, but veer very slightly over towards the right boundary. Ahead in the top boundary you should be able to see a waymark post to the right of a metal gate – go through onto a lane and turn right. The lane climbs past 'Long Mynd View' and into the village of Wentnor. Ignore a turning left after the Church to find The Crown a short distance further on. ❷

WENTNOR. *Described by Arthur Mee as 'A windswept village under The Long Mynd' it certainly feels the effects of the winter weather, being built on a small plateau above the River Onny, which affords it little protection. Despite that rather chilling description the village has a pleasant aspect with attractive stone houses lining its main street and it does have enviable views over the most superb hill country in practically every direction. The church of St. Michaels and All Angels is well worth a visit; it was restored in the mid-nineteenth century but has much older roots going back to Norman times and contains many interesting artefacts. Of particular interest might be the 'Hurricane Tombstone' which tells the story of a storm which struck Asterton in 1772 sweeping away a house and killing seven people.*

Whilst in the pub bear in mind that there is still some walking (and some climbing) to do so don't put yourself totally out of action. On leaving turn right and continue past the turning to Prolley Moor and Medlicott. After another a quarter of a mile you reach a point where the lane bears sharply left at a junction, with a narrower lane going ahead uphill. Take the narrower lane then, literally after 10 yards, go right through a gate into a field and follow the mixed tree boundary on your right. It kinks right and descends to the bottom where you go round to the left.

After 50 yards cross a stile on your right into the adjacent field with a hedged boundary on the left and at the bottom of this field go through another gate and continue the line forward to the left of a field boundary. In another 70 yards or so go ahead through a further gate onto a gravelly track to the left of Moorhouse Farm and, on the far side of it, continue on the track to exit through a gate onto a narrow lane. ❸

Bear left here and after 200 yards, just before the lane swings right, you come to Yew Tree Cottage with a waymarked metal gate to the right. Go through this onto a stoney track and, at the rear of the cottage, continue ahead in a field to the right of two more cottages. Cross a ditch and fence stile at the top to proceed ahead in the next field with tree boundary on your left and at the top is another ditch and stile. Having negotiated these and the following field there is a further fence stile to cross before exiting onto another tarmac lane where you turn left in front of the architecturally intriguing Stanbach Cottage. ❹

This quiet lane meanders an attractive way for about three quarters of a mile along the base of the western slope of the Long Mynd to reach a junction at Medlicott. Turn right at this point up a narrow lane signed 'No Through Road'. This is a fairly steep climb which takes you through a gate and on past the now derelict Medlicott Cottage. The surface has now become stony and there are excellent views over hill country to the right.

Keep going and on reaching more level ground where the post and wire fence ends, keep right at a fork on the unfenced track. I say 'more' level ground by way of comparison with what has gone before but the way continues upwards until you reach a crossroads at the top. You may recall this point as one passed on the outward route from the left and you bear left to retrace your steps for about half a mile back to the start.

SHORTER WALK

STARTING from The Crown, point 2, follow the main route to point 4 and the junction with a lane in front of Stanbach Cottage. Turn right passing Laburnum Cottage and continue on this gently undulating lane ejoying the extensive views across the Shropshire Hills to your right. Where the lane bears sharp right signed Prolley Moor and Wentnor, continue straight ahead along a 'No Through Road'.

Ignore a bridleway and buzzard waymark in 200 yards on your left and stay ahead to pass a small farm cottage and outbuilding after which the surface becomes stony. Go through a metal gate onto what is now a green lane before arriving behind Fir Tree Farm. Branch off right here to go to the right of a barn and the farm buildings and continue along a stony drive. On emerging onto a lane turn right and in 200 yards you reach Poplar Farm on your right. Now pick up the long route from here, just after point 1 and return to Wentnor.

12
Aston Munslow

FACT*file*

MAPS: Landranger 137; Pathfinder 931

DISTANCES: 7¾ Miles; shorter walk 3¼ miles

MAIN START: At the picnic site car park situated about 1½ miles east of Westhope on a lane running along the southern slope of Wenlock Edge. It can be approached from the north or west via lanes off the A49, otherwise the best route is probably a turn left off the B4368 3½ miles east of Craven Arms or, from the opposite direction, turn right 1½ miles after passing The Sun public house at Corfton. This is a lane which is signed Westhope and Ticklerton and it takes you some three miles directly to the start point providing you do not bear left into the village of Westhope. GR 479875

Public Transport: None.

SHORT START: The Swan at Aston Munslow on the B4368 about six miles north west of Craven Arms. GR 513866

Public Transport: Limited services 156 (Sats only) from Ludlow; 712 (Mon and Fri only) from Bridgnorth, stopping at Aston Munslow .

TERRAIN: A scenic walk on the slopes of Wenlock Edge with a descent into Corvedale to the villages of Aston Munslow and Diddlebury. Superb views along the route; some climbing on the return leg but well worthwhile. Walk at any time.

THE PUB: The Swan is reputed to be the oldest pub in Shropshire (1350). It certainly looks fairly ancient with its black and white timbered exterior and internal age-worn features. Dick Turpin was said to have stayed there, and on one of the walls is the story of Alf who called at the pub at six in the morning – a week later he was still there paying for his beer but getting his bread and cheese free! Normal free house range of ales and bar snacks. Beer garden.
Normal opening times but closed Monday lunchtimes, except on Bank Holidays.

TURN left along the lane for about a third of a mile through pleasant scenery of rolling hills and rural settlements. The lane descends to a junction where you turn sharp left towards Middlehope on another lane along which you climb for about 200 yards to arrive at a gateway on your right leading onto a driveway to a cottage. As the driveway sweeps left to the cottage, branch right through a gate onto a broad track. This winds through more scenic countryside – the epitome of Shropshire at its best – and eventually loops left through a gate or over a stile before continuing a gentle rise through a belt of (mainly pine) trees. You can see

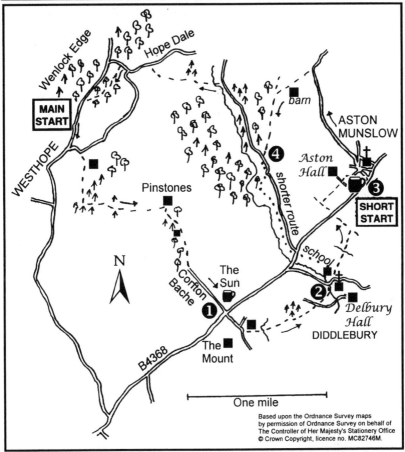

Based upon the Ordnance Survey maps
by permission of Ordnance Survey on behalf of
The Controller of Her Majesty's Stationery Office
© Crown Copyright, licence no. MC82746M.

Callow Hill a little closer now over to your right and little farmhouses nestling in the valley below.

Go straight over at a crossroads of tracks and round a left hand bend to pass through another area of pine trees to emerge via a gate which at the time of my visit bore the notice 'calves, cows and bull'. Continue forward keeping to the left hedged boundary and after about 150 yards where the grassy track swings right, bear left through a metal gate with marker tape. Follow the right boundary in the field and go through a gate, then another in a crossing boundary heading towards farm buildings.

You come to a cottage where there is a footpath diversion notice posted and we now follow the diversion by continuing ahead to a gate immediately in front of the farm buildings. Go through and turn almost 180 degrees right through the adjacent gate onto a metalled track. You don't walk along this for long however and bear almost immediately left onto a grassy path which leads around the rear of a livestock enclosure to Pinstones Farm.

Continue forward in a field to the right of the hedged boundary. Then start to descend on a course which overlooks a large barn conversion complex below. You pass through a gap in a crossing boundary above the far end of the development, then branch half right down the slope of the field to level ground at the rear of the buildings onto a stony track going away from them. This is the end of the diversion and the track follows an attractive route through a valley where wild flowers can be found in profusion in springtime and copious amounts of bracken in summer.

You pass a small quarry on your right and come to a crossing boundary of mixed trees, at which point proceed directly ahead on a broad enclosed track. After 150 yards go though a gate in front of a dwelling to exit onto a narrow tarmac lane by the said dwelling. Continue forward on the lane through the cottagey settlement of Corfton Bache until reaching a junction with the B4368. **❶**

If you can resist the temptation of early refreshment at the Sun Inn, or even if you can't, cross the main road directly onto another lane. You pass a splendid stone built residence and continue past a left turn for 100 yards or so to reach Beechwood Cottage. At the rear of it go through a waymarked kissing gate with the Georgian manor house of The Mount to your right. Go through a second kissing gate into a field and cross it in a direct line slicing off the left corner to reach a gate in the tree line on the opposite boundary. A brook crossing will bring you into the next field but do not keep tight on the left boundary – instead move away from it at an angle of about 25 degrees up a slope and continue to the top right corner where you will find a waymarked gate to the right of a plantation.

Go through, bearing right, then left through another gate after 20 yards and follow the hedged boundary to the plantation for the short distance until it kinks left. A little directional care is called for now – from this point carry on straight forward through parkland aiming roughly to the right of Diddlebury Church ahead. The line is not absolutely critical and after crossing the driveway to Delbury Hall you may need to make an adjustment to the right, to avoid what might seem the obvious route down a sunken path, in order to find a stile to the right of a mixed tree and hedge line (at the point where it joins a post and wire fence).

You are now in front of Delbury Hall. Cross the stile into a field following the left fence line on a downward course but, before reaching the bottom where there are some barn conversions, divert slightly to the right over a stile and footbridge then cross a further stile onto a narrow path bordering a brook. This shortly exits onto a lane in the village of Diddlebury where you turn right up to St. Peters Church. **❷**

DIDDLEBURY. *Of Saxon origin the name of the village denotes the 'burgh' or settlement of Duddela, an early English noble. Ownership passed to Edward the Confessor, Roger of Montgomery, the Abbey of Shrewsbury and, more latterly, the Baldwin family to whom memorials are placed in the church. It is another picturesque rural village with some interesting buildings and farmhouses. The ancient church is dominant and of great interest to architects and historians.*

Opposite the rear of the church bear left up a tarmac driveway leading to a school. After about 30 yards go through a waymarked gate to the right of the school buildings. You will cross a stile which takes you across the school playing field to another stile on the far side where there is a choice of routes. Take the one straight ahead in a field following the left boundary, cross a stile at the end of it and continue forward over a footbridge and stay on line with the hedge across another field towards the tree lined top boundary where there is a further waymarked stile. This exits onto a track and you turn left onto it ignoring the stile opposite.

The track can get boggy but after about 250 yards exits at the main road again. At the junction is a plaque to say that the Corvedale Byways and

Approaching Aston Munslow

Bridleways Group was awarded second prize in the Esso 1994/5 footpath awards to recognise achievements in working to improve access in this area. Cross the road directly onto a narrow upward path between hedgerows. After a stiff climb of about 200 yards look carefully for a stile on your right which leads into a field.

Cross the field directly to a driveway and negotiate a further stile opposite into another field. Bear very slightly right to another stile on the opposite boundary with good views of Brown Clee and other hills to the right. Cross this and the next field to negotiate further stiles on opposite sides of a driveway to Aston Hall and into a paddock. Cross the paddock to a stile opposite leading onto a narrow track to the rear of a garden area out onto a gravelled driveway which in turn leads to a junction with a lane. Bear left now for about 60 yards to another junction and turn right down to The Swan. ❸

The Swan, Aston Munslow

ASTON MUNSLOW. *In common with many other Shropshire villages these days Aston Munslow is a combination of farming and commuter communities. In addition to the historic Swan Inn (see Factfile) there is a rural museum called The White House which, like the pub, dates from the fourteenth century and is open to the public at certain times. The Methodist Chapel is the only non-conformist place of worship still used in the area.*

Over indulgence will be regretted, as there is now a stiff climb to face! Turn left, retracing your steps up the lane past the earlier point of entry onto it and past The White House. A distance of almost a mile will bring you to a point where the lane swings right through a gate and here bear left through a timber gate onto a broad stony track. A look backwards will make the effort of getting here worthwhile with a panorama over Brown Clee, Titterstone Clee and surrounding hills. Continue onwards until arriving at a barn and take the narrow path to the right of it as it carves through a field to a gate at the end. Go through and turn left onto a crossing track which descends gradually to reach a junction with a tarmac lane. **4**

Turn right up the lane with views over Hall Coppice and Hazeldine Coppice to the left and the valley below. The lane starts to drop down into Hope Dale and you pass an old quarry on the right with super views over the valley to the left with a river flowing through it. About 80 yards after passing a fir plantation on your right, branch left along a broad earth track which is known as Dunstan's Lane. You will shortly go over a ford and are then obliged to cross a dam at the end before picking up the left boundary to continue forward on what can be a muddy track which rises between hedgerows.

The track levels out to pass another small fir plantation and you go through a couple of gates about 60 yards apart before exiting onto a narrow lane. Turn left and on reaching a junction continue ahead towards Eaton and Ticklerton. It passes between trees onto Wenlock Edge and after some 200 yards goes into a left-hand bend. On this bend look carefully for a narrow path going off left uphill through trees and follow this as it levels off and loops right on a twisting course. Keep ahead at a junction with a wider track and stay on the well-defined route back to the starting point.

SHORTER ROUTE

FROM The Swan, point 3, turn left up the lane and, ignoring all side roads, follow it in an upward direction past The White House and pick up the long route through to point 4 and the junction with a lane. Turn left here and after about 80 yards there is a stile to cross on your right which takes you onto a path between trees. Instead of doing this you can cheat a little by continuing on the lane until it meets with the B4368 – but I'm sure such an idea will be dismissed immediately! So, avoiding temptation, go along the path and cross another stile into a field, following the edge of it to go through a gate at the end.

Now bear half left, going gradually downhill towards cottages below. At the bottom bear left onto a narrow path to the rear of a cottage before passing through a gap in a crossing boundary. At this point bear half right down an embankment to a stile to the right of another cottage and turn left on a track passing in front of it. Continue on this up its junction with the lane you were previously on and turn right for about a third of a mile down to the B4368.

Turn right to walk along the footpath for 20 yards before passing through a waymarked gate in the hedge on your left. Follow the hedged boundary and houses on your right and after crossing the third stile by a dwelling, another stile immediately to the right of it will take you across a sports field towards Diddlebury and St. Peter's Church (point 2). When ready, pick up the long route from point 2 (which will involve retracing your steps across the sports field, at which point you might see that you could have done a little more cheating!) and follow it back to The Swan.

13
Chelmarsh

FACT*file*

MAPS: Landranger 138; Pathfinder 932

DISTANCES: 6 miles; Shorter walk 3¾ miles

LONG START: At pull-in by Hay Bridge about 3½ miles south of Bridgnorth on the B4555. GR732888

  Public Transport: Bus service 125 Bridgnorth/Kidderminster stopping at Chelmarsh. It is suggested that you plan the walk starting from the village rather than walking the mile or so to the starting point at Hay Bridge.

SHORT START: At the Bulls Head just south of Chelmarsh Village. GR723875

  Public Transport: As above.

TERRAIN: Generally easy going on well-marked paths. One longish gradient on the second part but this is fairly gradual. Mainly open country with good views over Chelmarsh Reservoir and the Severn Valley. Some paths across fields, mainly on the second part, may be planted in summer and others could get overgrown. Be sure to take a stick but perhaps May-August best avoided.

THE PUB: On a clear day the Bulls Head commands extensive views over the Reservoir and surrounding area. It is a welcoming pub with three bars and wood burning stoves (the latter probably greatly appreciated on cold winter days when the wind blows across the reservoir). Banks's is the main ale on offer but Marstons, Guinness and various lagers are also available. Bar snacks are excellent value and there is a cosy restaurant if you want something more substantial. *Normal opening times.*

WATCHING out for traffic, turn right to go round a bend, under the railway bridge and over Mor Brook bridge to cross a stile on your right into a small field. Walk over the private driveway to Astbury Hall (not visible from this point) and go ahead up a grassy embankment to cross a stile at the top. Now cross the field facing you, slightly to the right towards farm buildings where a further stile brings you onto a track. If the field is cropped you may wish to consider walking around the edge. Turn left here, negotiate a stile by a farm gate and, on reaching the B4555 again, cross it to enter a tarmac bridleway almost directly opposite. Follow this for about a quarter of a mile before turning right up a drive to Dinney Farm and, on reaching it, bear left along a wide track in front of the house. ❶

After passing the farm buildings the track becomes grassy and you go through a waymarked gate after which superb views open up over the reservoir. If you have binoculars you may be lucky enough to spot grebe,

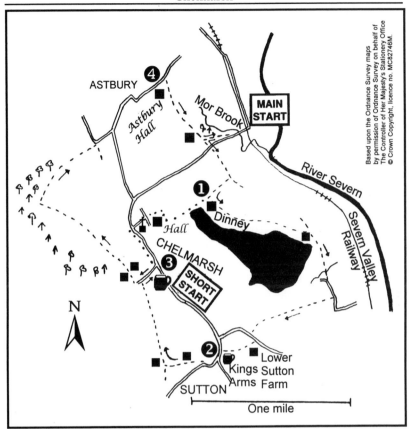

Based upon the Ordnance Survey maps
by permission of Ordnance Survey on behalf of
The Controller of Her Majesty's Stationery Office
© Crown Copyright, licence no. MC82746M.

Chelmarsh Reservoir

tufted duck, cormorant and other species. The reservoir is part of the River Severn Supply Scheme for joint use by Staffordshire Waterworks Co. and Wolverhampton Corporation and was formed in 1968. Water from the Severn is pumped up from an intake at Hampton Loade.

Follow the boundary with a fence on your left and after passing through a gate in a crossing fence your way is straight on aiming to the left of a line of trees on the brow ahead. Go through the bridleway gate just above the boathouse, and then take the waymarked gate to your right onto a grassy track. You may have noticed the 'Jack Mytton Way' markers – so named after an eccentric Shropshire character who lived in the early part of the last century and known as 'Mad Jack'. Renowned for his practical jokes he turned to drink and got into debt, was put in a debtors prison and died penniless in his late thirties.

The track descends to cross a stream and rises again up before you join and continue ahead along a tarmac drive. Go over a cattle grid and after a short distance you reach a point just before the drive bends right where there is a sign saying 'Caution concealed driveway', facing away from you. Turn right here through a gate into a field and go directly ahead to a gate in the opposite boundary. Now bear slightly right to aim for a hedgerow on the horizon ahead and continue with it on your right to pass through farm gates. There is an excellent view of the reservoir at this point with the boathouse in the distance.

Press forward on a stony track for a third of a mile before going through a gate onto a lane. Turn left for 100 yards then bear right over a stile adjacent to the entrance to Lower Sutton Farm into a field. Keep parallel to the left boundary to reach a stile on the opposite boundary and once over this turn half right towards the Kings Arms pub where there is another stile in a fence at the bottom of the car park. ❷

If in need of sustenance already you can take a break here, otherwise emerge onto a lane and follow it round to the other side of the pub and turn right along another lane signed Billingsley (Covert Lane). Follow for a short distance until reaching the second turn on an S-bend and bear right over a waymarked stile. On a clear day you get a good view from here of the Clee Hills ahead. Now aim to the left of two electricity poles towards a third pole on the far boundary to cross a stile. Again, this field was cropped at the time of research.

Surprisingly you will now find yourself on the edge of a lawn in front of a house. Do not be deterred! – cross the lawn and gravel drive to a gate opposite which gives access into a small paddock and a stile in the facing boundary. Enter a field and go straight ahead and over another stile just to the left of a white cottage. Turn right along a straight track and follow it for about half a mile over alternate surfaces of grass and rough tarmac. You will come to a junction with a lane opposite a group of houses called 'The Glebe'. Turn right here up to the Bulls Head for a well earned breather. ❸

When suitably refreshed and ready for the second leg, retrace your steps down Bakehouse Lane to where tarmac ends and turn right around to the rear of 'The Glebe'. Take a little care here and do not follow the track where it bends to the left; instead continue straight ahead to the left of a house to a gateway leading into a field just before Barland Cottage. Follow the field edge with a fence on your left and cross a stile into the next field, continuing on line to cross a further stile onto a farm driveway. Turn left towards buildings but before reaching them look for a double stile on the right which will bring you into another field. Follow the left boundary, cross yet another stile and turn right into the next field.

After 70 yards negotiate a stile by a farm gate bringing you onto a broad grassy track between hedgerows. Here there are pleasant views over open countryside with the Clee Hills again visible in the distance. On passing through a farm gate you will find you're facing a large field with no obvious route across. Do not follow either boundary but proceed diagonally over the field aiming for the opposite corner to the right of a tree to find a gate. Go through and cross the centre of another field heading to the right of a line of trees coming in from the left where there is a stile.

Cross the stile and continue the same line towards a further stile immediately to the left of a tree in the opposite boundary and, once over this, bear half right skirting the edge of a tree line towards the diagonally opposite field corner. You pass through a gate between two trees and veer left to follow the field boundary around and up a slight rise with a hedge on the left. Cross a stile and continue the gradual climb to the top where the boundary kinks right then left to reach a stile onto a grassy track. Walk down the track, which may be overgrown in summer, and after a short distance you will reach a junction with a farm gate on your left. Go through this and turn right down a partially surfaced farm track. After 200 yards bear left on a lane for half a mile into the hamlet of Astbury. ❹

You will pass Astbury Hall and some delightful stone cottages before reaching Astbury Lodge. A few yards further on turn right over a stile by a gateway into a large undulating field alongside Astbury Hall. Please do not be deterred by the rather unfriendly notices by the stile, just keep to the public path across the field which is clearly marked. The waymark points to the right of a small hawthorn tree just ahead to follow a line parallel to and a few yards away from the driveway to reach a stile in the far corner but there are further waymarks to guide you.

Once over the stile turn left along the driveway for 75 yards and then branch right following a waymark across a field towards trees and a further stile. After crossing you will arrive at some farm buildings and pass to the left of them along a grassy track. Then cross the farm drive and turn immediately left over a stile (or through the gate if the stile is overgrown – as it was, very severely, on a last visit) into a field. You should now recognise this as a field crossed on the outward route and follow the last short section in reverse back to the starting point.

SHORTER WALK

FROM pub car park turn left along the B4555 for 300 yards into Chelmarsh Village. Carefully cross the road and enter the churchyard of St. Peters.

CHELMARSH. *The origins of the village were founded on mining, cider making and brick manufacture as well as farming. A shallow mine shaft is still visible on the common and it is said that the ghosts of miners can be seen walking down to it at certain times of the year! St. Peter's church, which unfortunately is normally kept locked, dates from the fourteenth century and legend has it that there is a monk's heart buried high in the east wall. If you are fortunate enough to find the church open do go inside. There is some fine woodwork in the chancel and elsewhere, carved, so we understand, by local youths towards the end of the last century under the instruction of the vicar who ran wood carving classes for them. There is also a unique first world war memorial plaque containing photographs of the young soldiers and sailors from the village who were killed in that conflict.*

Chelmarsh Hall is also of fourteenth century origin and was the home of the powerful Mortimer family. It was formerly a granary and connected to the church by an underground passage.

Proceed around to the rear of the church and exit onto a lane opposite Church Cottage. Turn right and as the lane bears left after 100 yards take the waymarked path on your right onto the Jack Mytton Way alongside outbuildings to Chelmarsh Hall. At a junction bear right along a path which provides good views of the reservoir and on reaching another junction with a broad track turn left downhill. The track descends on a worn sandstone bed and flattens out to pass between railing fences at the end of the reservoir. You are in fact much closer to the water here than at any point on the main walk, which is great if you're a 'twitcher'. Ascend to Dinney Farm (point (1)) and turn sharp right on the track passing in front of the house (not the path immediately in front of it).

Now follow the long walk through to point (3) and back to the Bulls Head.

14
Enville to Six Ashes

FACT*file*

MAPS: Landranger 138; Pathfinder 932 & 933

DISTANCES: 8¾ miles; shorter walk 3¾ or 4½ miles

MAIN START: Public car park at the rear of the Post Office in Blundies Lane, Enville which is situated on the main A458 Stourbridge-Bridgnorth road, two miles north-west of Kinver. GR 825868

   Public Transport: Limited service 580 (Thurs/Sat) from Wolverhampton to Enville.

SHORT START: Whilst it is possible to construct a short walk from Six Ashes, I have to say that the more spectacular scenery is to be enjoyed from the Enville end and I have therefore chosen to start both the main and short walks from there.

TERRAIN: Varied, starting with a wander through the Enville Estate followed by a little climbing over the scenic Sheepwalks then cross country to Six Ashes. Return via farmland and a section of the Staffordshire Way.

THE PUBS: An attractive Olde-Worlde black and white building **The Six Ashes** has a friendly ambience and a comfortable interior. It was originally a farmhouse and there is a plaque on the bar wall telling something of its history during the last 167 years. There is a bar and lounge serving Bank's, Fosters, Guinness, Kronenberg plus Bulmers and Strongbow Cider. Good food menu. Beer garden.
Normal opening except closed Monday lunchtimes.

The Cat Inn at Enville is also very olde-worlde with a great atmosphere, particularly if you are a real ale enthusiast. The extensive 'menu' includes the locally brewed Enville Ale, Theakstons XB, Guinness, Carling, Christies, Strongbow and Stowford Press Cider as well as the Guests, which at the time of my visit were Devon Glory, Sarah Hughes Dark Ruby, Old Cat Astrophic and Beacon Bitter. There is even a whisky of the week and a vast array of Country Wines to tempt you. Good food menu.
However, please note that due to Enville Estate regulations the pub is not open on Sundays! Traditional opening times apart from this.

FROM the car park walk down to the main road and turn left along it for 150 yards or so before turning right up the driveway to Enville Hall, alongside The Cat public house. You go through a gateway then by some Estate cottages and follow the driveway past an athletic club to reach the Hall in its attractive parkland setting (Staffordshire Way).

ENVILLE. *An ancient parish with Saxon roots and meaning 'level plain' after the level valley in which most of the village is situated. It now serves as a commuter village for the commercial centres around Dudley and*

Kidderminster but retains a quiet unspoilt charm. The Hall dates from the eighteenth century and is the home of the Earls of Stamford. In 1904 it was badly damaged by fire and substantially renewed internally – it was probably this time when the roughcast rendering was put on over the brickwork and which, in my view, does not improve its attractiveness as a building. The parkland was created by William Shenstone of Halesowen, a local poet and landscaper. The Estate extends in all

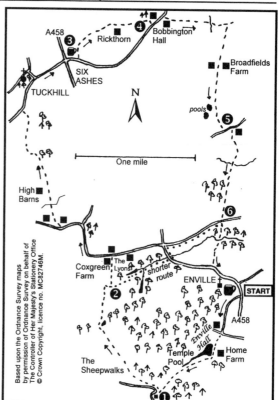

Based upon the Ordnance Survey maps by permission of Ordnance Survey on behalf of The Controller of Her Majesty's Stationery Office © Crown Copyright, licence no. MC2746M.

Enville Hall from Temple Pool

to around 7500 acres and in the last century kept 35 men and boys employed.

On arriving at the end of the stable block, with the drive to the Hall going up to the right, leave the tarmac and go over the large stile directly ahead into a pasture field. Cross the field on the same line to reach a waymarked stile 150 yards ahead on the far side, where there is a good view backwards to the Hall.

Cross the stile onto a path which runs beneath trees to the left of Temple Pool, a beautiful and peaceful spot, especially in autumn when the colours are changing. The path goes under an arbour of holly trees to emerge alongside Home Farm and, at the end of the buildings, cross a stile then another after a further 50 yards. Now bear half right on a defined farm track which initially runs parallel to the tail of Temple Pool then joins a tree line on your right.

Temple Pool

Go through a waymarked gate and continue on the track through another gate to take the line of a waymark arrow climbing gently on a diagonal course half left to pass to the left of a lone chestnut tree. Stay on this general line across pasture (if you look right you may glimpse, hidden in the trees, a tiny deserted chapel although it was never dedicated as such) passing about 80 yards to the right of an oak tree, at which point you will see a house directly ahead. Aim towards it and you will arrive at a stile in a post and wire fence in front of a paddock ❶

DO NOT CROSS THE STILE but turn right to rise up pasture keeping the house and a lane on your left. You pass a waymark post after a few yards to reach the top of the field. Here cross a stile in a crossing boundary before bearing half right in the next pasture field on a diagonal course towards the tree line to find another marker post near the top of the rise.

There are super views from here on a clear day: backwards half left is the sizeable village of Kinver with the well known local beauty spot of Kinver Edge to the south of it (National Trust, well worth a visit – nice walks); directly backwards you may be able to see the outskirts of Stourbridge and Dudley, and slightly ahead left the town of Kidderminster in the distance. It has been said that these views and those on the Sheepwalks following are the best in South Staffordshire. This could well be true although no doubt there are some who would argue with it!

Stay parallel now with the tree line to pass another waymark post after which the way curves right to cross the Sheepwalks. You shortly pass a further waymark which takes you across the top of a deep gulley and continue on course with the waymarks until the ground starts to drop again and views open up in front over open countryside. From here on a clear day the Clee Hills can be seen. Incidentally, if you are wondering what the derelict building over on the left is, it is a long deserted shepherd's cottage.

Now start a descent towards the next waymark post located in the tree line below to the left of a pool some 150 yards ahead. Continue forward for a few yards to a further waymark and stile and cross the latter. You pass over a boggy bit of ground to arrive at a facing field and turn right to follow along the boundary. There is, or at least was, a notice posted here advising you that this is a Wildlife Conservation Area. The boundary initially runs to the left of the pool then rises away from it before dropping again. At the end bear left with the waymark onto a farm track but after only 20 yards go right through a gap in a hedge to follow the right boundary of the adjacent field. At the end of this field bear right with waymark along a narrow track between trees and after 100 yards another waymark directs you left to a stile in front of a facing field, with Coxgreen Farm in view over to the left. **❷**

If taking the main walk, cross the stile and the field directly aiming for a track visible between trees on the opposite side. The field may be cropped, in which case it should be possible to walk around the edge if this is necessary. Go along the track towards a cottage ahead to exit onto a lane in front of it. Turn left passing the entrance to Coxgreen Farm, after which the lane goes through a long right bend and then a left where you ignore the turning off to the right. The lane rises slightly and immediately after passing a new house on your right, and before coming to the next house, turn right along a waymarked path over a stile following the fence at the bottom of a private garden. Cross a further stile at the end of the garden and walk along the ensuing field boundary with High Barns Farm ahead.

At the end of the field cross a double fence stile with a tiny plank footbridge between and continue the line forward to the end of the next field where there is an awkward wide stile with a triple waymark. Take the option straight ahead into an area of ground which will be thistly in summer although you soon come out of it to cross another awkward stile, where the ground falls away at the base, then another after 30 yards parallel with High Barns Farm. In the next, longer, field follow the right boundary and cross a stile at the end onto a path which goes to the left of a small covert.

At the end of the covert you are diverted left around an enclosure of Christmas trees and, after about 40 yards, swing right keeping the hedge on your right as it departs from the enclosure. You come to a waymarked fence stile which is crossed into an undulating field keeping the tree boundary on your right. Nice views from here. Just before reaching the top of the field go through a metal gate on your right onto a green lane which shortly brings you to a junction with a tarmac lane.

Turn right on the lane to reach the settlement of Tuckhill after about a quarter of a mile. On your left is a wooded area which you can walk through to a nineteenth century church (Holy Innocent) hidden away in a beautiful spot in the trees. Unfortunately, like so many these days, it is kept locked. Continue on or return to the lane before passing a farm and turning right at a junction to arrive at the Six Ashes pub in about a quarter of a mile. ❸

When you can persuade your legs to function again, leave the pub and turn left along the adjacent lane. You shortly pass Orchard Cottage and then arrive at Honeysuckle Cottage where you follow the footpath sign through a gate across the drive and through the garden to reach a stile. Cross into a paddock and follow the left edge bearing left at the end through a gateway before turning right to continue more or less on the same line but now with the fence and tree line on your right. You cross a double stile on the right after 50 yards into a large field and walk along the left edge of it, passing to the right of a small wood after which you can see Gateacre Park Farm well to the left. At the end of the field cross a stile by a gate then another a few yards beyond into a facing field.

A little directional care is required now. You need to head across the field, or go round it if planted, towards a gap in the hedge line on the opposite side about 100 yards ahead. Do not be tempted to veer left towards a gap in front of a belt of trees. Go through into the next field with Rickthorn House ahead crossing directly to the left of the property. Again you may wish to skirt around the edge if cropped. Continue to the left of a barn to the end of the field where you go through a gate onto a broad grassy path to the right of a fir plantation towards another cottage. This brings you out onto a lane where you bear left. ❹

You pass the entrance to Bobbington Hall, a complicated looking property, and at the point where the lane enters a sharp left bend, branch off right over a waymarked stile into a field. Keep to the right boundary and cross a stile after 100 yards into another (long) field where the line is more or less straight across it heading towards the end of a line of trees on the far boundary. However, it is much more sensible to turn right and walk around the edge although the way could be nettly in summer. There is first a line of Poplars, then Willow – at the end of the latter cross a stile then a ditch into pasture following a ditched boundary on your left.

At the end of this field cross another stile in a wire fence followed by a plank footbridge over a brook and continue with the left boundary fence which shortly kinks 90 degrees left to a stile which you can see 150 yards ahead. Here there is a choice of routes. Cross the stile and bear right into the adjoining field with a hedge on your right heading towards Broadfields Farm and, at the end, exit through an opening onto a concrete driveway. Go through gates (or over if padlocked, as at the time of research) following the waymarked path between farm buildings and through another gate on the far side just to the left of the last barn. A waymark here directs you forward into a field with a hedge on the right.

Go through a gate in a crossing boundary and after another 100 yards you will need to cross a stile to continue the same line but now to the right of a barbed wire fence. At the end of the field cross another stile and bear very slightly left (the waymark is misleading as it directs you further left) across a field to a stile on the opposite boundary in front of some trees. Cross and walk over a short scrubby area before continuing in a field following the right hedged boundary. There are some pools on the right. At the end squiggle through a gap to continue forward now with the boundary on your left and this leads you down to a gate and onto a lane.

❺

Turn left on the lane then branch right after 150 yards along the Staffordshire Way to the right of a cottage. You cross a stile then veer left in a field with the boundary on your left. At the end do not go through the gate but bear right with the Staffs. Way sign along the bottom boundary of the same field to cross a stile after another 100 yards. Proceed along the left edge of the next field towards some trees where the path dips to the left down a short embankment to go through a gate and across a footbridge onto a narrow path between the trees. Exit via a stile to continue along the right edge of a large field, ignoring a stile immediately on the right. You shortly pass to the left of a wood with the path rising gently and negotiate a stile in a crossing boundary and then another shortly afterwards. Ignore a double stile on the right after the wood has ended and exit via yet another stile onto a lane. **❻**

Cross the lane directly over a stile following the left edge of a field. The way dips to go through a wooded hollow and over a footbridge and you come out the other side to continue with the Staffs. Way mark across a double stile on each side of a farm track. Proceed now on a narrow path between rows of trees to emerge via a metal gate to walk along the right boundary fence to another private garden. On gaining a road, the A458 again, turn left towards Enville. There is a grass verge but take care as the road is usually busy. After about 250 yards you reach the Church of St. Mary the Virgin which was restored by Sir Gilbert Scott in the early 1870s. It has a number of interesting features, including old stained glass, unusual carved stalls or misericords, organs and tombs. Continue along the road for about another 150 yards and bear left up Blundies Lane back to the start.

SHORTER WALK

FOLLOW the main route from the start through to point 2, the stile in front of a facing field. Cross the stile and turn right along a swathe of grass along the top edge of the field. You pass a line of trees and shortly join a hedge on the right with the rather splendid looking residence of The Lyons off to your left. The hedge line starts to curve gently round to the right after about 100 yards and at this point look for a stile on the opposite side of the narrow field on your left, more or less in line with The Lyons.

Cross the stile down an embankment above a stream but after a few yards bear round to the right on a narrow path running along the embankment. The path is marked but is uneven and could be overgrown in summer. After a short distance it rises again to join the fence line to the field and you soon have a pool for company below. It then winds through a copse bordering a brook to exit via a stile after which stay on line for about 25 yards before bearing left in front of a waymarked gate to cross the brook and continue on a more open path. You stay on this now until it arrives at a junction with the A458.

You can if you wish turn right and follow the main road for a little over half a mile to Enville Church then pick up the main route for the remaining distance back to the start. However, if you would prefer to cut down the main road walking at the expense of a little further distance, turn left along the verge and after a climb of some 200 yards turn right at a crossroads onto Morfe Lane, towards Swindon. Follow this now for about half a mile to a point where it rises slightly to a little crest, at the top of which is a crossing right of way with waymark posts on each side. This is point 6 on the main walk and you turn right to cross a stile onto the Staffordshire Way again and rejoin the main text to return to the starting point.

15
Stoke St. Milborough

FACT*file*

MAPS: Landranger 138; Pathfinder 931 (mainly) & 932

DISTANCES: 7 miles; shorter walk 3¼ miles

MAIN START: At Stoke St. Milborough – along the lane leading to the Church may be suitable if a service is not in progress. To get there from the Bridgnorth direction take a right turn off the B4364 Ludlow Road about two miles after passing through Burwarton. From the Ludlow direction, there is a left turn about 2½ miles after Middleton. GR 567823

> **Public Transport:** Limited service 142 (Wednesdays and Fridays) from Bridgnorth stopping in Stoke St. Milborough. Early morning service 716 runs from Ludlow on schooldays.

SHORT START: At the Three Horseshoes on the B4364 at Wheathill. GR 599819.

> **Public Transport:** Service 141/142 between Ludlow and Bridgnorth runs fairly often along the B4364 but the nearest stopping point is at Cleedownton, 1½ miles on the Ludlow side of Wheathill.

TERRAIN: Mainly waymarked paths around the slopes between Brown Clee and Titterstone Clee. Some climbing but stunning views make the effort well worthwhile. Walk at any time.

THE PUB: Very much a local pub with simple furnishings and quarry tile floor. An excellent walkers pub in fact. Ales include Burtonwood, Labatts, Forsters, Murphy's and Guinness. Modestly priced meals and bar snacks are sometimes available. A sign outside proudly offers "Sunday lunches our speciality – just like your mother's". I have a feeling that could be a deterrent in some cases!

Normal opening times.

STOKE ST. MILBOROUGH. *An attractive village on the southern side of Brown Clee and one of several 'Stokes' in Shropshire derived from a Saxon word signifying village or inhabited place. The church has a Norman tower but is mainly fourteenth century although of mixed styles due to considerable restoration over the years. It is named after St. Milburgha, the first Abbess of Wenlock Priory, who legend has it was pursued by men with bloodhounds until she fell from her horse. Needing water for her wounds she bade her horse strike the rock where she fell and a spring gushed forth! That spot was at Stoke St. Milborough and the spring still exists, having recently been restored. It is said to be a cure for eye complaints.*

FROM the village proceed northwards on a lane towards Clee St. Margaret. You will pass by St. Milburgha's well (entrance through a wooden gate on the left by a black water pump) and an old chapel, now the home of a firm of agricultural engineers with a pet cemetery in the front garden. Continue past the left turn to Cold Weston and a number of quaintly named cottages followed by farm buildings to arrive at a bend with a small parking area on the right. Go through a gateway into heathland signed 'Clee Liberty' and enter onto a broad stony track. After about 30 yards the stone surface ends and you are faced with a perplexing choice of grassy paths ahead.

Take the path to the extreme right which gradually moves towards a hedged boundary with a field and continues parallel with it in a direct line towards Brown Clee summit ahead. Don't panic – the walk does not involve an ascent of Brown Clee – instead enjoy the magnificent scenery around the county's highest landmark at 1722 ft. Did you know that during the last century it also had the highest coalfield in Britain? Indeed it was at that time the centre of much mining activity but has still managed to retain an extraordinary natural beauty. The hedged boundary gives way to a line of hawthorn trees. Keep tight on these and follow a narrowing green track around to the right, climbing gently.

Views of Titterstone Clee now open up on your right and you come to an unoccupied cottage called 'The Sands' with a warning to trespassers posted on the front wall. The cottage has a grinding wheel and a water pump but no visible means of vehicular access which bears witness to the

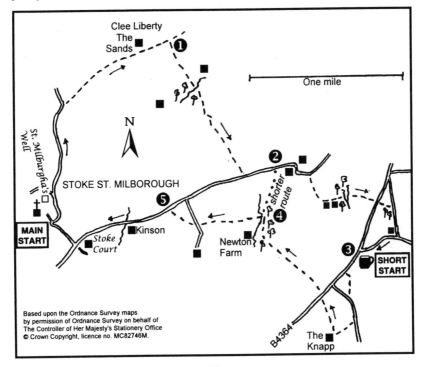

lifestyle of its former occupants. It also has an unusual weather vane on its roof depicting a hunt scene. After the cottage the track widens out into moorland around the foot of The Clee and you continue the line forward with a tree line on the right, still climbing gently. After about 300 yards, just before a large beech tree you will arrive at a stile on your right. ❶

Cross the stile and follow the Shropshire Way with a line of hawthorn trees on your right and Titterstone Clee ahead. Now familiar for its visually prominent radar station, Titterstone Clee was also mined for coal and ironstone during the last century. You can still see the incline plane built to take the material down to Bitterley Yard, full trucks providing the momentum for the empty ones going up. Cross a further stile with an isolated cottage off to the left and descend, still with the tree line for company. The path crosses a small brook and rises up an embankment to reach another stile to the right of a metal gate under a large oak tree.

After the stile the track undulates and twists and turns before straightening to arrive at a gateway giving access onto a narrow path between lines of trees. This path, which can be muddy at times, gradually descends to exit onto a lane. Turn left and walk along this pleasant lane as it dips and then rises fairly steeply. After about a quarter of a mile you will pass an old 'Tardis' type telephone box on the right just before a crossing right of way. ❷

Those on the short walk will approach this point along the path to the right and turn right along the lane. If following the main walk simply continue ahead through an S-bend passing Batch Cottage and Yew Tree Cottage and up a rise, towards the top of which is a waymark sign directing you right down a roughly surfaced bridleway. Titterstone Clee is again in the picture and panoramic views open up on the right. Ignore a turning on the left and continue on the track as it curves to the left. Ignore all stiles and pass in front of a stone built cottage with a pretty timbered outbuilding and dovecote at the rear. When you reach a second cottage the track veers right but you continue forward along a grassy path between trees/hedgerow. This descends onto a narrower and sometimes muddier path to arrive at a stream. Cross both arms of the fork in the stream up an embankment on the far side to pass through a wicket gate at the top.

Continue on the track as it rises gently and go through another wicket gate and into a field following the mixed tree boundary on your right. You exit via a timber gate onto the B4364 and cross it directly to go over a sort of a fence stile then a small platform stile passing to the left of farm buildings along a hedged field boundary. The ground around these stiles was found to be overgrown at the time of research. The hedge turns to trees as you border a small copse and you exit via a platform stile onto a lane. Turn right here and get prepared for a superb view to the left over the Shropshire Plain towards Bridgnorth. At a T-junction by a farm bear right and as you round the bend further views open up over surrounding hill country. You reach the main road again with the Three Horseshoes on the left. ❸

When, or if, the urge prevails, leave the pub and turn left along the B4364. Ignore the entrance to the first caravan site after 20 yards but after another 200 yards or so, go left through a barred gate by the sign 'Caravan Club Members Site' and onto a gravelly track. This leads you through a further gate into a field which you cross diagonally to a gate in the right hand corner onto a lane. Turn left and walk along the lane as it dips and rises. Part way up the rise branch off right at the entrance to Knapp Farm along a waymarked track. You are now back on the Shropshire Way and are as close to Titterstone Clee as you will get on this walk, its 'mushroom' radio station being more clearly visible.

Just before reaching the farmhouse follow the waymark sharp right across the adjacent field to a stile ahead in a crossing fence. Once over, bear half right towards a further stile visible to the left of a corrugated metal roofed building. It will become apparent as you near the building that there is a cottage adjoining it, secluded in the surrounding trees. Cross the stile onto a roughly surfaced driveway which exits onto the B4364 again. Turn right then immediately left following a waymark and sign to Newton along a broad straight track. Eventually the track dips and bears around to the right past Newton Farm to enter an area of trees with a brook below on the left. Keep a sharp lookout now for a fence stile in a gap in the hedge on your left just before the track bears left and rises. If you start climbing you have gone too far – unless you are doing the short walk that is. ❹

The fence stile is crossed into a thicket – be careful as there is a bit of a drop down on the other side. Turn right and down to cross a footbridge and climb an embankment on the far side. Now keep left through a cluster of hawthorn and beech trees to emerge into an open field, where you follow a line parallel with the tree boundary on your left. Go through a gap in a crossing boundary and forward in the next field keeping parallel to the hedge on your left. Newton Farm can now be seen again further below to the left.

Cross a fence stile in the top left corner into the next field and follow the left boundary for 25 yards until the trees end and a post and wire fence begins. Here bear very slightly right, just clipping off the field corner to a fence stile in a crossing boundary and, once over this, continue the line slightly right to the top right corner of the adjacent field where there is another fence stile by an oak tree. Cross this and proceed in another field with a hedged boundary on your right. Just where it kinks left there is yet another fence stile to cross beneath a holly tree.

Cross the next field directly to a further fence stile 100 yards ahead and onto a lane. There is a drop down to a ditch on the far side so take care. Almost immediately opposite cross another fence stile (keep telling yourself this is good for the leg muscles!) into a field and veer half right across it to a stile visible in the boundary ahead. This stile exits onto the Stoke St. Milborough road and you need to turn left along it. ❺

The pleasant lane winds past Kinson Farm adjacent to which is the site of the medieval village of Kinson, although there is not a lot left to see. After passing a new Village Hall you reach a T-junction by Stoke Court and turn right back to the village. Before doing so however, look to your left for a tableau which details the location of various places of interest in the area. Over the adjacent wall is a pretty pool which looks to be the remains of a former moat. The lane meanders back through an attractive residential area passing a converted school house dated 1856 before returning you to the start point.

SHORTER WALK

FROM the pub at point at point (3) follow the long route to point (4) but here continue ahead on the track as it rises up a short hill to pass a cottage on the right. The track deteriorates to earth and grass to exit onto the lane at point (2). Now join the long route again through to point (3) to return to base.

16
Wyre Forest

FACT*file*

MAPS: Landranger 138; Pathfinder 932 & 952
DISTANCES: 10½ miles; shorter walk 4½ miles
MAIN START: At Kinlet, on the B4363 about nine miles south of Bridgnorth and 4½ miles north-east of Cleobury Mortimer. GR 717803

Public Transport: Bus service 125 Bridgnorth/Kidderminster stops at Kinlet and Highley. Train: Severn Valley Railway only to Bridgnorth or Highley, which is four miles to the north-east. (enquiries 01299 401001).

SHORT START: The Button Oak at the place of the same name on the B4194, three miles south-east of Kinlet and 3½ miles north-west of Bewdley. GR 752782

Public Transport: Bus service 125 stops at Buttonoak and Bewdley. Train – as above or from Bewdley where the S.V.R. also stops.

TERRAIN: A pleasant combination of open farmland and mixed forest. One or two gradients but these are not too arduous. Walk at any time although it is possible that some planting or overgrown paths may be encountered in the summer.

THE PUB: A charming walker friendly pub with a good atmosphere. Serving Banks's, Guinness, Harp, Draught Strongbow and Grolsh plus Guest Ale. Bar snacks, meals and beer garden.
Normal opening times except closed Monday lunch.

KINLET. *In the south-west corner of the county and close to the Hereford & Worcester border, the village of Kinlet has royal connections with Edward the Confessor, or more precisely, Edith his wife who was sister to King Harold. The name Kinlet is derived from Old English words meaning 'royal' and 'district' although the oak forests which then covered the area have long since been removed, largely for ship building timber. Mercifully, the nearby Wyre Forest remains, even if many of the oaks have been supplanted by conifers. A curious feature is that the village layout does not conform to the normal pattern of houses built around the church. The village was actually moved in the eighteenth century by the Lord of the Manor in order to create a park, thus leaving the church in splendid isolation in the grounds of Kinlet Hall. Powerful people these feudal Lords! The church is really quite striking as is the Hall itself, which is now a private school.*

START along the main road towards Bridgnorth and just beyond a row of semi-detached houses bear right onto a tarmac lane signed 'No Through Road'. You pass by Kinlet C of E school, go through a gate and turn immediately right along the edge of a field bordering the school playground. Continue through a gap in crossing boundary into the next field and keep going alongside the hedged boundary to exit via a gateway onto a lane where you turn left.

After about a quarter of a mile (there is no footpath so beware of traffic) the lane rises to reach the entrance to Catsley Farm on your left. Go along the drive towards the farm and, as you reach it, branch right in front of a barn to go through two gates in quick succession before bearing left into a field alongside the rear of the buildings. Keep to the left boundary to pass through two gates in crossing boundaries into a field which rises gradually to reach a fence stile just to the right of an enclosed paddock adjacent to the top corner. Cross and turn right following the right boundary of a field and cross another fence stile heading towards the houses of Buttonbridge. You join the boundary fence of one of the houses (Buttonbridge House, as you will see shortly) and exit via a stile onto the B4194. ❶

Turn right and after about 60 yards cross the road and go over a waymarked stile into the bottom end of a large garden to a private residence. Stay close to the bottom boundary and cross over a short section

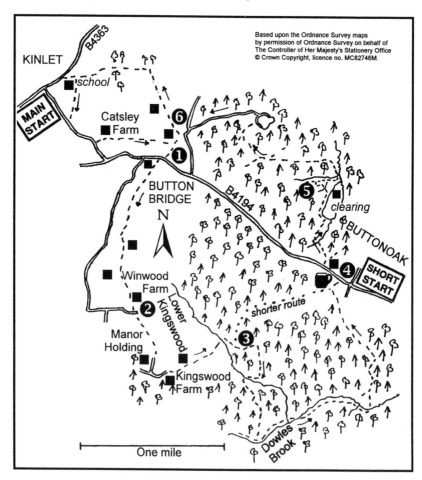

of lawn to a stile to the left of a line of conifers. Once over, cross a large pasture field directly to a stile you can just make out on the far side in a line of trees. Cross this and the one opposite into a small field with a post and wire fence on your left heading towards farm buildings. You go through a gate in a crossing boundary, then bear diagonally right to walk around two sides of a large paddock to cross a fence stile in the right corner. (followers of the O.S. map will note a departure from the definitive route here, the paddock diversion being seemingly a permissive path)

Go over the next small field to another fence stile which leads onto a short grassy path, over a crossing track and a small metal stile into a field at the rear of the farm buildings where you follow the holly boundary on your left. Cross a stile in a crossing boundary and another at the end of the next field with farm buildings off to the right. Go through a gate to continue forward with a hedge on your right and, after a while, Winwood Farm comes into view ahead. You go through another gate to join a track heading towards the farm and follow it as it passes to the right of the buildings and takes you through a metal gate adjacent to a barn before arriving a crossing track, which is the farm driveway. **❷**

Go over and up the grassy track opposite and through a metal gate. Ignore a waymark directing you left after 100 yards and continue ahead to go through a further gate into a field with the tree lined boundary on your left. In 50 yards you go through another gate to follow the same line but now with the boundary on your right. On arriving at a crossing hedge go through yet another gate to follow the footpath sign ahead for 50 yards to cross a stile leading onto a narrow hedged path. After 100 yards or so it opens out onto a lane at Manor Holding and you continue ahead to a junction where you turn left to follow the lane as it curves left past a bungalow and up to Kingswood Farm.

Go through a gate and onto a track between the farmhouse and barns and stay with it as it gently winds down to Lower Kingswood Farm. Here take the green lane to the right of the farm gate and climb gently to the right of the buildings before dropping down again between hedges. A further 50 yards brings you to a gate into a field where you keep close to the right boundary along traces of a wide green track.

At the next boundary the line ahead is blocked so take the gate to the left along the adjacent field with the hedge on your right. You will then be able to go through a gap in the hedge on your right to resume the line of the green lane. At the end you cross a fence stile and the following field diagonally to the lower left corner. Continue to descend for about 20 yards through rough scrub, ford a brook and negotiate a fence stile before emerging onto a track leading uphill. A climb of about 200 yards or so will bring you to a point where the ground levels out and there is a waymark post with a track coming in from the left. **❸**

Those on the short walk will join the route here and bear left onto the track but, if you are following the main walk, continue ahead through a beautiful mixed plantation of fir and deciduous trees. You will shortly reach a waymark post in a small open area where you fork right and continue along this track for about 200 yards to another waymark, just where the track curves left. Here you turn off right to pass between two fenced clearings. On arriving at a crossing track after another 150 yards or so turn right onto a track which follows a course above a stream. It veers sharp left to cross the stream, then rises to meet a crossroads of tracks where you bear left on a path which passes through a clearing. Keep to the path and you will reach a stone forestry road which you cross directly onto a narrow path and stay on this until it descends to meet a broad track alongside Dowles Brook.

WYRE FOREST. *All that remains of a huge forest which stretched from Bridgnorth to Worcester but it is still one of the largest surviving ancient forests in the country, covering over 2,600 hectares. In the last century it was a centre for coppicing with much of the harvested oak saplings being burnt for charcoal for use in iron smelting. Pit timbers were also supplied and there was a trade in oak bark which was used in the leather tanning process. The town of Bewdley grew from this forest trade and many of its buildings have associated names; for example, The Royal Forrester and The Colliers Arms. Dowles Brook, along which you will now walk, was a source of water power with a number of corn and felt mills having been built along its route. Today, the Brook valley is rich in flora and fauna, as indeed is the forest generally, part of which is a National Nature Reserve. There is a lot more I could tell you about this beautiful place but space does not permit – pick up a leaflet or two from the Tourist Information Centre at Callow Hill.*

Turn left onto this track, ignore the fork right to a footbridge after 150 yards but a few yards further on bear left onto a broad forestry road. Stay on it for maybe a quarter of a mile before the track takes you across a stream to a T-junction where you turn right onto a narrower track (ignore the left turn before a stream crossing). You shortly cross Dowles Brook via a footbridge and follow a very attractive way above and beside the brook for around half a mile before bearing left at a fork by a Forestry Commission sign to cross another stream and continue on a uneven path by a Wyre Forest National Nature Reserve sign. After initially rising, the path soon descends to cross a footbridge and, once over, continue ahead for 70 yards then bear left at a T-junction. After only 50 yards branch right at a fork to go through another fenced clearing, then turn right after a further 200 yards at a crossroads.

Follow this track now for almost half a mile until you come to another crossroads where you continue ahead, ignoring a track coming in from the left after a few yards. A few yards after that, bear right at a fork then left at another fork after 30 yards just by an open field. Stay on this track now for about a quarter of a mile until you meet a broad swathe of a track coming in from the left. It will not take a genius to work out that this track has been widened for a specific purpose – it is a section of the line of the

The Button Oak

pipeline carrying water from the Elan Valley to Birmingham. Just to your right is a stile which you cross into a field which adjoins a paddock containing various types of livestock. You will cross a fence stile at the end onto the B4194. Turn left and The Buttonoak is immediately on your left.

Assuming you can manage to motivate yourself towards the exit door, leave the pub and turn left along the road for about 200 yards to the point where it bears left and branch off right along a broad metalled track alongside timber Forestry Commission houses. At the rear of the houses you reach a fork and branch off left on a broad track which after a while dips to cross over a brook, then rises to meet gates in front of a prohibited area.

Turn right here on a track which initially follows the fence line alongside the enclosure and then takes you through pine trees to arrive at a clearing. Look ahead here and you will see a house on the other side of the clearing – this will shortly become a reference point. Turn left along the edge of the clearing and a distance of about 300 yards will bring you to a bridleway post and a path off to the left, almost at the point where you draw level with the house referred to. Take this path which initially drops to cross a stream, then rises gently to meet a crossing track. Bear left and then right after another 40 yards on a track which drops to a junction with a broad track running parallel with a gulley and stream. ❺

Turn right onto the track which runs along the top of the gulley and crosses it to continue around a left bend with the brook below now on your right. On coming out of the bend branch left at a fork on a track which winds gradually upwards for about a third of a mile to arrive at a crossroads. Cross directly and after about 250 yards bear left onto a metalled forestry track with the prohibited enclosure off to the left.

In a further 40 yards branch off right along a similar track and then bear right again after another 300 yards or so along a narrower track just before a left hand bend. Bear right again after a further 60 yards before the track starts to descend more steeply on a path which falls gently as it winds through the trees and soon emerges into an open area with holiday chalets, cottages and a secluded pool. Cross a short grassy area to join a road and turn left, dropping down in front of some stone and wood clad bungalows. The road swings right, then left, to leave the clearing via a lane which you follow for about half a mile on a gradual ascent to reach a public lane at the top where you turn left. **❻**

After 100 yards the lane veers left but you bear right following a waymark along a broad stony track to the right of Dormer Cottage. The surface turns to tarmac and reaches an isolated cottage where you cross a stile to the right of the entrance gates. This takes you into a field and you follow the hedged boundary around it. Both Titterstone Clee and Brown Clee are visible from this point. At the end of the field cross a small metal fence section in a crossing boundary and continue the line in the next field to the top, where you bear left through a timber gate in front of a small wood.

The line is now directly across a field keeping about 150 yards to the left of the right boundary and aiming to the left of a grassy hummock where the ground dips down to the right. If this field is planted it should be possible to work a course around the edge. Beyond the hummock is a gate in a tree line which leads onto a track from which you emerge and continue ahead along a field edge with its boundary on the right. Exit the field by Kinlet School and retrace your steps back to the starting point.

SHORTER WALK

FROM The Button Oak, point 4, turn right to cross a stile into the field alongside the pub garden. You will pass a paddock containing a variety of animals and birds before crossing a stile at the end to enter upon a broad swathe of land which cuts upwards through the forest. It will not take a genius to work out that this track was cut for a specific purpose – it is in fact the line of the water main carrying water from the Elan Valley to Birmingham and at the top of the climb you will pass a large chamber in the centre of the swathe.

After another 300 yards cross over a stone forestry track and continue a gradual descent for another 150 yards to reach a waymark post directing you left down a narrower track into the trees. The way can be muddy at times as you wind down through pine trees. Ignore a path to the right and then another shortly afterwards on the left into a prohibited conservation area. The ground levels out and descends again to bring you to a crossing track at point 3. Turn left here and then follow the long route back to point 4.

17
Hopton Castle

FACT*file*

MAPS: Landranger 137; Pathfinder 950

DISTANCES: 8¼ miles; shorter walk 4¼ miles

MAIN START: The village of Hopton Castle, where there is verge parking either side of the telephone kiosk. From Craven Arms take the B4368 towards Clun but bear left at Purslow along the B4385 and after two miles there is a right turn into Hopton Castle. GR 364782.

  Public Transport: Service 736 (Thurs only) from Ludlow calling at Hopton Castle. If you are dependent upon public transport you might do best travelling by train to Bucknell (Shrewsbury/Swansea line) and starting from there.

SHORT START: The Baron of Beef at Bucknell which is to be found on the north side of the village going out towards Clun. Approached from the Ludlow direction via the A4113 and a right turn some 3½ miles after passing through Leintwardine. From Craven Arms take the B4367 down to Leintwardine. GR 353741.

  Public Transport: As above. Service 736 also stops at Bucknell.

TERRAIN: A superbly scenic but quite strenuous walk through woods and across hill country, with excellent views. Be prepared for some stiff climbs but, rest assured, the effort is worthwhile. Walk at any time of the year but do not attempt unless you are reasonably fit.

THE PUB: The Baron of Beef is an attractive stone built property which looks as though it may have been converted from a former farmhouse. It is quite food oriented but there is a locals bar where you should feel comfortable in walking boots. A good selection of ales is available including M&B, Worthington, Caffreys, Guinness, Carling and various guest beers. At the time of my visit the choice was between Jawbreaker and Dorothy Goodbody!
Normal opening times and open all day from noon on Sat/Sun.

HOPTON CASTLE. *A small, rural village which, not surprisingly, owes its name to a castle belonging to the de Hopton family. All that remains now of the twelfth century structure is a ruined keep situated on a mound at the west end of the village. During the Civil War it was owned by one Robert Wallop, who withstood a siege by Royalists despite being vastly outnumbered but was finally forced to surrender. Although negotiating terms for the lives of the men to be spared, they were all butchered, with the exception of the Governor. The Church of St. Edwards was rebuilt in 1870 following a fire which destroyed the original church which dated from the tenth century. Worth a visit if you have time.*

G O out of the village in a westerly direction passing the church over to the right. After a short distance, as the lane swings right, go through a gate on your left onto a broad stony track. You pass through two more gates heading towards the woods of Hopton Titterhill and the path bears left to a further, somewhat dilapidated and possibly

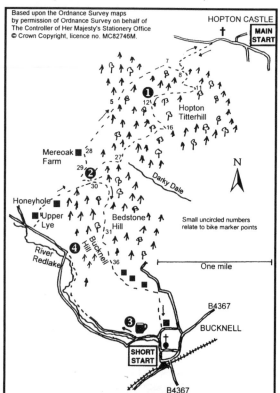

padlocked, gate in front of the wood. Go through onto a grassy path which loops left around the bottom edge of the wood and arrives at a junction after about 120 yards.

Turn right here uphill and in another 100 yards or so look for mountain bike marker post No. 8 on the left. If you reach post no. 7 a little further on you have gone too far! The woods of Hopton Titterhill and Bucknell Hill to the south, a total area of some 860 acres, have been laid out by the Forestry Commission as a mountain bike trail and the marker

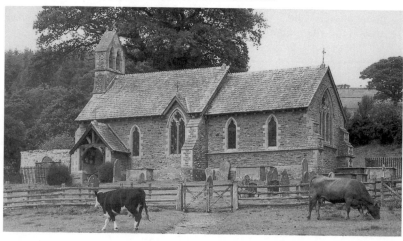

Church of St Edwards, Hopton Castle

posts are our route guide for the early and later stages of this walk. Don't get the idea that the area is saturated with bikers careering around all over the place – this is certainly not the case. I only saw one.

Bear left at post 8 to continue an upward course which zigzags over an area of loose shale and up onto a track climbing steeply into the wood. On arrival at post 11 you need to almost double back sharp right to continue the climb on a stony track to a point where it again doubles back, this time to the left. Go with this (do not take the track straight ahead) and in a few yards you join a higher track where you go right, again almost doubling back. A further 50 yards will bring you to post 12, at which point turn left to leave the stony track in favour of another one. ❶

The track rises to cross Hopton Titterhill and there are magnificent views to the rear over Purslow Woods and Clunton Hill. You eventually make level ground and start descending with more superb views ahead over Bucknell Wood, Brampton Bryan Park and into Herefordshire. Continue your descent to reach a broad stone crossing track and marker 16. Here turn right, then left, on a track falling steeply down to the left between two groups of beech trees. The path narrows to drop steeply and sometimes slipperily down the hillside. At marker 27 you join a wide track curving round in front of you and bear right onto it. Follow this now for perhaps a little over a third of a mile to reach marker 30, where there is a four-way junction and a Forestry Commission sign. ❷

Bear round to the left and take the second broad stony track on the left which sweeps around to the left then rises to the right of Bedstone Hill. The track levels and descends gradually to meet a junction by marker 31. From here continue ahead, over a crossing track after 50 yards and onto a grassy path heading uphill alongside Bucknell Hill. The path rises to a summit then immediately drops with panoramic views all around and you arrive at a junction by marker 36. Proceed ahead now along a stony track to exit from the wood. You pass by a cottage then descend past another with the quaint name of 'Heavens Above' with the village of Bucknell now in view ahead. Eventually the track becomes metalled and you carry on past Willow Cottage to reach a junction with a lane going left and signed Mynd and Bedstone.

At this point bear 90° right through a gate into a field (i.e. do not go onto the lane) and follow the right hedged boundary. You are shortly funnelled into a sunken track still following the right boundary but with a line of hawthorn and ash trees on the left. Go through a gate at the end of the field and continue line forward downhill but now with the next field boundary on your left. Proceed forward across a gap in a hedge line towards a house ahead keeping to the left of a large oak tree to pass through a gate to the left of the house. This exits onto a lane after 30 yards and here you turn right. Turn right again at junction by telephone kiosk, past a modern housing estate then a farm to arrive at the Baron of Beef. ❸

BUCKNELL. *A large village with twelfth century origins and nestling in a valley close to the intersection of borders between Shropshire, Herefordshire and Wales. Its prosperity increased in the mid nineteenth century with the opening of the railway station on the new Heart of Wales Line and it became a bustling community with several shops, four pubs, a corn mill and numerous trades providing employment. Although the coal depot still operates, the station is no longer manned and most employment is found in the nearby towns or in agriculture. The village is laid out in a square pattern with the remains of a motte in its centre. The church of St. Mary is mainly fourteenth century and has an unusual blue enamelled clock.*

The Baron of Beef, Bucknell

Getting into gear again may take a little effort but, fortunately, there is a relatively flat section to start you off. Turn right on leaving then immediately right again up Bridgend Lane. After passing by a few cottages you are joined by the River Redlake on the left. There are more properties on the other side with gardens sweeping down to the riverbank. You will pass a house called Redlake Reach and a few fairly classy residences. Ignore a footbridge on the left and stay on the lane as it goes past Hill House and take the gate to the side of it onto a grassy path. Another gate will lead you onto a narrower path through pleasant fringe woodland between the river and the base of Bucknell Hill.

The path becomes more elevated and winds a very attractive course above the river and you pass along a section with a steep embankment to the left as you head towards the wood in front. You don't go as far as the wood however; after the embankment look carefully for a stile on the left at the bottom of a short drop which gives access into a field. Cross the field more or less directly to meet the river again (the line is not critical) and look for another stile adjacent to it. Negotiate this and follow the course of the river as it twists and turns to arrive at a gateway exiting onto a lane to the right of a stone bridge. ❹

Bear right on the lane which quickly swings left and stay on it for about a third of a mile. Upper Lye farmhouse will come into sight to the half right, set back from the lane up a rise. Turn right up the steep tarmac driveway to the farm and, on reaching the buildings, continue ahead up a grassy embankment to the right, through a gate and upwards on the same line. At the top of the ascent go over a stile and ahead onto a grassy track. You pass to the left of the cutely named 'Honeyhole' and cross a stile by a gate and another about 100 yards on.

Press forward on an upward path in a field to the left of a wooded area and, right at the end of the field, go through a kissing gate to emerge again at point 2 which you passed through on the outward route. Now double back to the left along a grassy track which swings right after about 150 yards and continues to the left of the trees. Another 150 yards or so will bring you to a junction with a broad stone track and marker post 29.

Branch left onto the broad track and go through a gate towards Mereoak Farm. Keep right at a fork to pass to the right of the farm buildings and then bear right at marker post 28 through a gate onto a broad stony track on relatively level ground. Superb views open up on the right over the Shropshire/Hereford border and, after a while, you are joined on the right by a young plantation of conifers before reaching a crossroads at marker 5. Go directly ahead over the crossroads onto a grassy path (not the track uphill to the right) which rises slightly then starts to descend.

Keep left at a fork after 200 yards to continue descent and take care as the path is fairly steep and can be slippery in wet conditions. Again magnificent views present themselves ahead over Purslow, Clunton etc. and, when you reach the bottom at marker 7, turn right onto a broad track. You shortly pass marker 8 on the right which was a turning point on the outward route. After another 100 yards bear left to exit the wood and retrace your steps back to base.

SHORTER WALK

FROM the Baron of Beef, point 3, follow the long route through point 4 and on to and through the kissing gate to bring you out at point 2. Now pick up the main walk text from point 2 and follow this back to the start, but of course, from this direction you need to turn right onto the broad stony track referred to which sweeps round to the left.

18
Caynham and Hope Bagot

FACT*file*

MAPS: Landranger 137; Pathfinder 951

DISTANCES: 7½ miles; shorter walk 2½ miles

MAIN START: In the village of Caynham, 2½ miles south-east of Ludlow on the road between Ashford Carbonel and Cleehill. Approached from Ludlow via the A49 or the A4117 if travelling from the east. Parking spaces are restricted and the best place is the small lay-by next to the telephone kiosk. GR 552731

 Public Transport: Nothing suitable.

SHORT START: The Bennetts End Inn and The Penny Black located between the villages of Knowbury and Hope Bagot, off the same Ashford Carbonel-Cleehill road and about 1½ miles south-west of the latter. GR 582745

 Public Transport: Very limited service 723/724 from Cleobury
 Mortimer to Knowbury.

TERRAIN: A scenic walk in the shadow of Titterstone Clee, including picturesque villages, churches and a former prehistoric hill fort. Walkable at most times although some paths may be overgrown or planted over in the summer.

THE PUBS: Yes, plural! Two pubs adjacent to each other and they are as different as chalk and cheese. Originally one establishment but now operated separately, they offer the visitor an intriguing choice of venue.

The Bennetts End Inn is much the older with a quaint interior comprising bar, lounge and restaurant. Ales include Tetley, Ansells, Guinness, Carlsberg and Carling. There is a pleasant beer garden. *Traditional opening times.*

The Penny Black is relatively modern with a comfortable interior and serving a good range of ales including Worthington, Guinness and Carling, plus Strongbow and other ciders. Bar snacks and meals available.

The pub is closed on weekday lunchtimes except at Bank Holidays.
I hesitate to say try them both, unless you are on soft drinks of course!

CAYNHAM. *The parish of Caynham includes the villages of Knowbury and Cleehill, where indeed the majority of its 1,000 or so residents live. These communities were founded on the Titterstone Clee stone quarrying industry although Caynham itself is much older with a mention in the Domesday Book and, even earlier, there was a bronze/iron age settlement to the north, but a little more of that later. In the Middle Ages the manor was owned by the powerful Mortimer*

98

family, and the parish church of St. Mary is the most obvious survivor of this period. The hamlet now falls within the influence of Ludlow although it is still very much reliant on agriculture.

FROM Caynham turn westwards towards Ludlow then left down a lane signed Greete and Tenbury. On the corner is the site of the village pound where stray cattle were kept until their owners were traced and fined. You pass through a small, pleasant residential corner before crossing Pervin Bridge to take the waymarked gate immediately after it on your left. Climb gently in the field to skirt the right edge of a tree line with a brook below to your left. Go through a gap in a crossing hedge then keep close to the tree line to exit through a wooden gate and scramble down an embankment onto an unmetalled lane. Turn right and proceed up a gentle rise to the left of a black and white cottage and to the right of another

cottage then cross a stile by a gate into a field. There is a grassy track over the field which takes you directly ahead to a metal gate in the far hedge and there you cross a stile to the left of it.

Continue the line ahead with a hedge on your left, then a line of oak trees, before crossing a field directly on the same bearing to a stile in the opposite hedge. Cross into the next field and continue ahead to the right of a solitary oak to reach a stile in the opposite boundary.

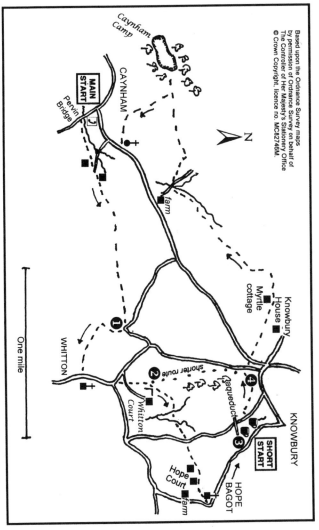

Once over press on along a faint path across a ridge to cross a stile in the far boundary to the left of a gate. Continue ahead in the next field directly towards the far left corner and go through a gate. Now strike out half right across a meadow towards the opposite corner to a stile exiting onto a metalled lane. **❶**

Turn right and in 15 yards right again onto a farm track and follow it as it meanders muddily between hedges. Look for a stile alongside a metal gate on your left after some 250 yards and cross into a field. Follow the left hedged boundary and negotiate a stile in a crossing boundary taking in the superb vista over the Shropshire/Herefordshire border; cross another stile and continue the line forward still following the left boundary along the top of a sloping field. The settlement of Whitton comes into view with only the silo spoiling its timeless ambience. At the end of the field is a gate and stile between dwellings which leads onto a short enclosed track exiting onto a lane opposite St. Mary's Church.

If time is short or the pub beckons, turn left along the lane which climbs steeply then levels out to arrive at a right turn by a post box. Alternatively, go up the steps opposite to the church, an interesting mixture of Norman and fourteenth century architecture with an unusual doorway which stands on its own with no tie to the main structure. Unfortunately it is kept locked due to vandalism – a sad reflection of current times. Also sad are the remains of a Celtic cross outside the entrance. Retrace your steps onto the lane and turn right up to the post box. There is a third choice – divert right into Whitton with its beautiful Jacobean style manor house, barn conversions and pretty cottages, then take the path opposite the manor up to the church.

Take the waymarked gate to the right of the post box, through a kissing gate and cross the field directly to a fence stile opposite. Whitton Court comes into the picture, a splendid residence which is largely obscured from view. Cross the driveway to it and go over another fence stile and on into another field, bearing very slightly right to reach a double stile beneath a tree in a crossing boundary to the left of the walled garden to the estate cottages. **❷**

Once over, continue bearing slightly right to pass the corner of the walled garden and then ahead across open pasture to a gap in a stone wall on the opposite boundary. A look backwards will be rewarded with wide views across a vast expanse of countryside. In the gap is a rather awkward fence stile to cross into a field, from where you can see clearly the settlement of Cleehill ahead. Now follow the right walled boundary which drops quite steeply into a valley where there is a brook. You are obliged to negotiate the brook before crossing a stile in some trees, and in the next small field continue forward to cross a footbridge over another brook, after which bear left to follow the line of it. After about 40 yards, where the brook starts to meander left, continue the line forward across a pasture field diagonally to a waymarked stile in the top right corner.

You exit onto a very narrow lane, turn right then immediately left over a stile which shortly leads to another with a choice of routes. Proceed forward for about 15 yards and take the left option around the field edge, but soon start to move away from it to pass a large single oak to reach a gateway to the front left of a large new Georgian style house with the much older Hope Court behind. The gate is located about 60 yards from the left corner of the field – go through into another field to the rear of the property following the timber post boundary, through another gate and onto a broad track which runs to the rear of Hope Court. It curves round towards Hope Court Farm and, as it straightens and the laurel hedge on your right ends, go through a gap opposite into the adjacent field (if you go just beyond the gap there is a waymark on a gatepost facing the other way).

Cross the field heading slightly right towards the right side of Hope Bagot church. You arrive at a stile and exit onto a lane where you turn left.

HOPE BAGOT. *Derived from the tiny medieval manor of 'Hope' which was held under Mortimer by the 'Bagard' family. The church (St. John the Baptist) is well worth a visit – it is substantially Norman with some later additions and of considerable architectural interest. Unfortunately parts of the structure are now suffering from the ravages of time. The churchyard is a sanctuary for wildlife. If you go though a gate at the rear and turn left you can visit what is described as a 'holy well' which was once visited by pilgrims seeking a cure for eye defects. It is situated under a massive yew tree which is reputed to be over 1600 years old and must be a good 8ft in diameter.*

The lane is a little steep but soon levels out and you reach the pubs where on the left you can see an aqueduct carrying water from the Elan Valley to Birmingham. ❸

I hope that the opportunity to sample two pubs together will not render you totally incapable of completing the walk! If not, go to the rear of the Penny Black car park and find a narrow path leading off downhill along an embankment above a brook. Cross a footbridge and stile and short field to the right of a cottage with the aqueduct off to your left, to cross another stile onto a lane.

Turn right and after 15 yards go left over a stile and short section of field and through a gate to turn 90 degrees right following a tree boundary on your right. You climb gently and pass by some cottages and go through a gap in a crossing hedge. From here turn half right following the line of telegraph poles to cross a rather crude fence stile 80 yards ahead in a hedged boundary. Climb into the adjacent field turning half left to cross it diagonally aiming to the right of a modern detached house close to the top right corner. Here you will find a gate exiting onto a lane. ❹

Turn right in a residential area and after 80 yards go left over a waymarked stile and follow the left conifer boundary to a new private house to exit onto yet another lane. Cross the lane directly over another stile and proceed in a field following the left boundary. Go over a further stile and another at the end of the next field with Knowbury House to your right. Continue along a path at the bottom of an orchard and over a double stile to continue on the same line. Towards the end of the field you need to veer off right up the slope away from the left boundary to a gate in the end boundary. Do not go through a gate in the bottom corner in front of Myrtle Cottage. You are led into a field at the rear of a belt of trees and keep to the left boundary to exit onto a broad metalled track. Continue ahead onto it but ignore the sharp left to Myrtle Cottage before entering a grassy track to the left of another property and proceed through a gate ahead (not the one on your left) into a field following the left hedged boundary. There are good views from here over into Herefordshire towards Richards Castle and also Ludlow in the valley below.

At the bottom of the field take the left of two gates into the adjacent field with the boundary on the left and go through a timber gate at the end. Bear right and go through another gate after 50 yards to continue the line forward to pass through a further gate at the end of the next field. Proceed ahead still following the left boundary through yet a further gate and, at the end of the next field – just for a change – there is a stile. Cross and bear half right passing to the right of a chamber over water pipes from the Elan Valley. You meet a line of trees on the far boundary bordering a brook and bear left to follow them along the bottom edge of the field. At the end cross a stile onto the entrance drive to a farm and turn right over a bridge across the brook to go through metal gates onto the stone driveway leading away from the farm.

Now, be careful here – please do not proceed along the driveway for more than about 10 yards before departing from it to cut half left across the adjacent field, roughly bisecting the angle between the drive and the left boundary fence, aiming towards the right end of the hedge line on the top boundary where there is a stile about 30 yards in from the end of it. When the field is planted the farmer marks the way across, or at least he had at the time this walk was researched.

Cross the stile and turn right following field boundary as it curves left, and at the end of the field, cross another stile and bear half left up the slope of the next field cutting off the right side. Go through a gate in the top boundary and cross the next field to go through the right hand of two gates on the opposite side. Continue the line forward diagonally across the next field to the top right corner in front of trees encircling Caynham Camp. Go over a stile then another on the opposite side of a driveway to enter Caynham Camp.

This outstanding landmark covers an area of about eight acres and is of bronze/iron age origin. Excavations in the 1960s revealed evidence of occupation from around 1000BC. More recently it had been used by the Romans, then Cromwell as a base for his siege of Ludlow. After looking around retrace your steps diagonally across the field and go through the gate, but now turn right on a downward course following the right hedged boundary. At the bottom go through a gate and continue forward but now with the boundary on your left. You go through another gate and proceed towards farm buildings but, after 50 yards, cross a fence stile on your left

Titterstone Clee from Caynham Camp

by a dead tree stump and cross the adjacent field towards Caynham Church. At certain times of the year there may be a path trodden across the field. Cross a stile in front of the churchyard and turn right. The church is unfortunately kept locked for security reasons. Exit by the lych gate and turn right on the road to return the quarter mile back to the start.

SHORTER WALK

FROM the pub(s), point 3, follow the long route to point 4. Here turn left to walk through a pleasant residential area and after about 200 yards, having passed the last house, cross a waymarked stile on your left into a long field. Once over the stile, bear half right diagonally across the field and cross a fence stile just to the right of the left corner into the next field. Keep the same line across it to reach a rickety gate in a brick wall on the far side to the right of a clump of trees.

Go through into a pasture field with the cottages to Whitton Court now in view over to the left and, again keeping roughly to the same line, aim for the left corner at the end of the walled garden to the cottages where there is a double stile. You are now at point 2 but DO NOT CROSS THE STILE. Instead imagine that you have already crossed it from the opposite direction, pick up the long route at this point and follow it back to the start. It may not escape your notice that you will virtually double back on yourself here to reach the fence stile in the stone wall referred to – one of those occasional illogical diversions necessary to adhere to the right of way. It would have been simpler and quicker to cut across the top boundary of the field to reach the fence stile but this would have meant straying off the definitive route!

Index